The BIG ALASKA REPRODUCIBLE Activity Book!

BY CAROLE MARSH

This activity book has material which correlates with the Alaska learning standards.

At every opportunity, we have tried to relate information to the History and Social Science, English, Science, Math, Civics, Economics, and Computer Technology Alaska directives.

For additional information, go to our websites:
www.thealaskaexperience.com or **www.gallopade.com**.

Correlates with Alaska's
ACS
Content Standards

Published by
GALLOPADE™ INTERNATIONAL
800-536-2GET
www.gallopade.com

Reading

D1305859

Gallopade is proud to be a member or supporter of these educational organizations and associations:

 NSSEA

 **ASCD**

 ABA AMERICAN BOOKSELLERS ASSOCIATION

 AP&PL ASSOCIATION OF PARTNERS FOR PUBLIC LANDS **SUPPORTER**

 NCSS

A Word From The Author

Alaska is a very special state. Almost everything about Alaska is interesting and fun! It has a remarkable history that helped create the great nation of America. Alaska enjoys an amazing geography of incredible beauty and fascination. The state's people are unique and have accomplished many great things.

This Activity Book is chock-full of activities to entice you to learn more about Alaska. While completing puzzles, coloring activities, word codes, and other fun-to-do activities, you'll learn about the state's history, geography, people, places, animals, legends, and more.

Whether you're sitting in a classroom, stuck inside on a rainy day, or—better yet—sitting in the back seat of a car touring the wonderful state of Alaska, my hope is that you have as much fun using this Activity Book as I did writing it.

Enjoy your Alaska Experience—it's the trip of a lifetime!!

Carole Marsh

The Alaska Experience Series

My First Pocket Guide to Alaska!

The Alaska Coloring Book!

My First Book About Alaska!

Alaska Jeopardy: Answers and Questions About Our State

Alaska "Jography!": A Fun Run Through Our State

The Alaska Experience! Sticker Pack

The Alaska Experience! Poster/Map

Discover Alaska CD-ROM

Alaska "GEO" Bingo Game

Alaska "HISTO" Bingo Game

A Word From The Author

Alaska is a very special state. Almost everything about Alaska is interesting and fun! It has a remarkable history that helped create the great nation of America. Alaska enjoys an amazing geography of incredible beauty and fascination. The state's people are unique and have accomplished many great things.

This Activity Book is chock-full of activities to entice you to learn more about Alaska. While completing puzzles, coloring activities, word codes, and other fun-to-do activities, you'll learn about your state's history, geography, people, places, animals, legends, and more.

Whether you're sitting in a classroom, stuck inside on a rainy day, or—better yet—sitting in the back seat of a car touring the wonderful state of Alaska, my hope is that you have as much fun using this Activity Book as I did writing it.

Enjoy your Alaska Experience—it's the trip of a lifetime!!

Carole Marsh

Geographic Tools

Beside each geographic need listed, put the initials of the tool that can best help you!

(CR) Compass Rose   (LL) Longitude and Latitude
(M) Map   (G) Grid
(K) Map key/legend

1. _____ I need to find the geographic location of Germany.

2. _____ I need to learn where an airport is located near Fairbanks.

3. _____ I need to find which way is north.

4. _____ I need to chart a route from Alaska to California.

5. _____ I need to find a small town on a map.

Match the items on the left with the items on the right.

1. Grid system
2. Compass rose
3. Longitude and latitude
4. Two of Alaska's borders
5. Symbols on a map

A. Map key or legend
B. Canada and the Arctic Ocean
C. A system of letters and numbers
D. Imaginary lines around the earth
E. Shows N, S, E, and W

ANSWERS: 1-LL; 2-K; 3-CR; 4-M; 5-G; 1-C; 2-E; 3-D; 4-B; 5-A

The Lovely Forget-Me-Not

The wild forget-me-not (*Myosotis alpestris*) was adopted as Alaska's state flower in 1917. The beautiful blue flowers have yellow centers and can be found throughout Alaska. Forget-me-nots have a frail appearance, but they're actually hardy enough to survive the cold Alaskan weather.

This little poem was included on the legislation that designated the forget-me-not as Alaska's state flower.

A little flower blossoms forth
 On every hill and dale,
The emblem of the Pioneers
 Upon the rugged trail;
The Pioneers have asked it
 And we could deny them not;
So the emblem of Alaska
 Is the blue Forget-me-not.

Use the facts you've learned about the forget-me-not to answer these questions.

1. When was the forget-me-not adopted as Alaska's state flower?
   _____

2. True or False: Forget-me-nots may appear frail, but they're actually pretty hardy. _____

3. True or False: Forget-me-nots can only be found in a few areas in Alaska. _____

4. A _ _ _ _ was included in the legislation that designated the forget-me-not as Alaska's state flower.

5. According to the poem, who asked to have the forget-me-not made a state emblem? _____

If the state flower got mixed up with the state bird, what would you have?

A willow-me-not—it could happen!

Alaska Government

Alaska's state government, just like our national government, is made up of three branches. Each branch has a certain job to do. Each branch also has some power over the other branches. We call this system checks and balances. The three branches work together to make our government work smoothly.

A governor, lieutenant governor, and department heads make up the Executive branch of Alaska's government.	The Legislative branch is made up of the 20-member Senate and the 40-member House of Representatives.	The judicial system of courts includes the Supreme Court, Court of Appeals, Superior Court, District Courts, and Magistrates.
Executive Branch	**Legislative Branch**	**Judicial Branch**

For each of these government officials, circle whether he or she is part of the EXECUTIVE, the LEGISLATIVE, or the JUDICIAL branch.

1. Governor   EXECUTIVE   LEGISLATIVE   JUDICIAL

2. Lieutenant Governor   EXECUTIVE   LEGISLATIVE   JUDICIAL

3. Superior Court Judge   EXECUTIVE   LEGISLATIVE   JUDICIAL

4. Magistrate   EXECUTIVE   LEGISLATIVE   JUDICIAL

5. Head of Department of Tourism

     EXECUTIVE   LEGISLATIVE   JUDICIAL

6. State Representatives   EXECUTIVE   LEGISLATIVE   JUDICIAL

7. Supreme Court Justice   EXECUTIVE   LEGISLATIVE   JUDICIAL

8. District Court Judge   EXECUTIVE   LEGISLATIVE   JUDICIAL

9. State Senator   EXECUTIVE   LEGISLATIVE   JUDICIAL

10. Head of Agriculture and Commerce

     EXECUTIVE   LEGISLATIVE   JUDICIAL

The number of legislators may change after each census.

ANSWERS: 1-Executive; 2-Executive; 3-Judicial; 4-Judicial; 5-Executive; 6-Legislative; 7-Judicial; 8-Judicial; 9-Legislative; 10-Executive

All Around Alaska! Bubblegram

Let's take a tour of some super sights in Alaska! Use the Word Bank to fill in the Bubblegram below! Now unscramble the "bubble" letters to complete the mystery message.

WORD BANK

Fire Island	Sitka
Hoonah	Tanana
Hooper Bay	Teshekpuk
Mount McKinley	Tok
Mount Saint Elias	Unalaska

1. ◯ _ _ ◯ ◯ _ _ _ _

2. T _ _ _ _ _ _

3. _ _ _ _ _ _ ◯ _ _

4. _ _ ◯ _ _ _ _ _ _ _

5. _ _ _ _ ◯ _ _ ◯ _

6. ◯ _ ◯ _ _ _ _ _ _

7. _ ◯ ◯ _ H

8. ◯ _ _

9. _ ◯ _ _ _ _

10. _ _ _ ◯ ◯ _ _ _

Mystery Message: Alaska's nickname is

"_ _ _ _ _ _ _ _ _ _ _ _ _ ."

The Legendary Sourdough Expedition Rebus!

In the winter of 1909, seven miners or "sourdoughs" led by Tom Lloyd decided to climb North America's highest peak—Mount McKinley. Seven set out; none had any climbing experience. Three turned back. Billy Taylor, Pete Anderson, and Charley McGonagall joined Tom Lloyd in the ascent.

Use the rebus clues to complete these statements about the famous Sourdough Expedition.

1. This is what a "Sourdough" is. The term "Sourdough" referred to a miner or

    an [image] + [image] + er = _ _ _ - _ _ _ _ _ _, the opposite of a gr + [image] +

    n + [image] = _ _ _ _ _ _ _ _ _ _.

2. The name "Sourdough" came from the yeasty [image] + ter =

    _ _ _ _ _ _ _ used to make br + [image] + s = _ _ _ _ _ _ which were

    a [image] - r = _ _ _ _ _ _ _ part of the miners' diets.

3. The miners climbed, without ropes, while carrying a [image] + [image] =

    _ _ _ _ _ _ _ _ _ to plant at the summit. For 18 hours, the sourdoughs

    climbed up and up.

4. Remarkably, two men made it all the way to the top. Unfortunately, it was the

    north peak; the s + [image] - m + p + [image] - b =

    _ _ _ _ _ _ _ _ _ _ is actually higher.

5. The Sourdough X + [image] + e + [image] = _ _ _ _ _ _ _ _ _ _ _ _

    is still considered one of mountain climbing's most amazing [image] + s =

    _ _ _ _ _.

Wheel of Fortune—Native Alaskan Style!

The names of Alaska's native tribes contain enough consonants to play . . . Wheel of Fortune!

See if you can figure out the Wheel of Fortune-style puzzles below! "Vanna" has given you some of the consonants in each word.

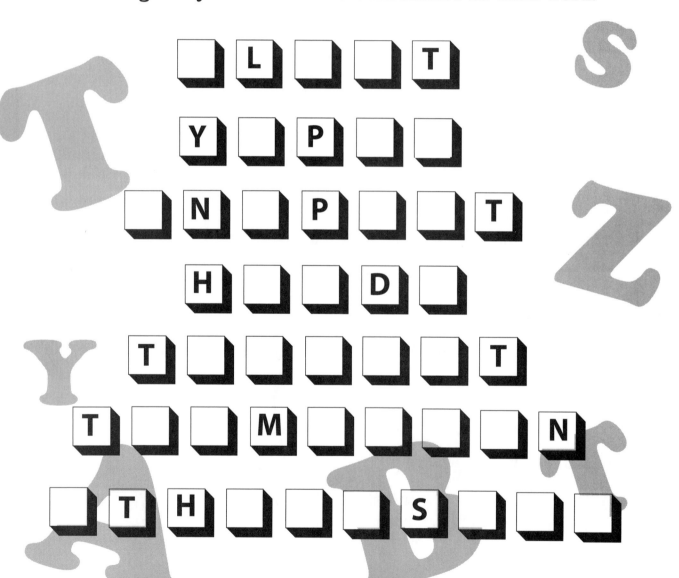

Rainbow, Pretty Rainbow

Alaska is "the place" for rainbows! Because of its northern location, Alaska is blessed with big, brilliant, beautiful rainbows! Rainbows are formed when sunlight bends through raindrops. Big raindrops produce the brightest, most beautiful rainbows. You can see rainbows early or late on a rainy day when the sun is behind you.

Color the rainbow in the order the colors are listed below, starting at the top of the rainbow. Then, in each band write down as many Alaska-related words as you can think of that begin with the same first letter as that color!

Rainbow Colors

Red
Orange
Yellow
Green
Blue
Purple

In the Beginning...

The Russians were the first explorers to arrive in Alaska. Czar Peter the Great sent Vitus Bering on a mission to the North Pacific to find out if Asia and America were connected by land. Bering crossed Siberia and sailed for America on the *Saint Gabriel* in 1728. In the spring of 1741, a second expedition with Aleksey Chirikov brought the Russians in search of America again! Bering's ship landed on present-day Kayak Island, dropped anchor, and the crew went ashore in July 1741.

Help the Russians find their way to Alaska!

During Bering's first expedition, he found the two continents were not connected.

Georg Steller, a member of Bering's crew on the *Saint Peter*, was the first explorer off the boat—the first to set foot on Alaskan soil!

ALASKA

Finish

Start

Throughout the 1700s, Spanish, British, and French explorers set out for Alaska in search of a trade route to Asia and new lands to colonize.

U.S. Time Zones

Alaska is divided into two time zones called Alaska Standard Time (one hour earlier than Pacific time) and Aleutian Standard Time (one hour earlier than Alaska time). Most of Alaska operates on Alaska time. Only the Aleutian Islands and St. Lawrence Island operate on Aleutian time.

Because of the rotation of the Earth, the sun travels from east to west. Whenever the sun is directly overhead, we call that time noon. When it is noon in New York City, the sun has a long way to go before it is directly over San Francisco, California. When it is 12:00 p.m. (noon) in Anchorage, it is 3:00 p.m. in Chicago, Illinois. There is a one-hour time difference between each zone!

Look at the time zones on the map below, then answer the following questions:

1. When it is 10:00 a.m. in Juneau, Alaska, what time is it in California? _____ a.m.

2. When it is 6:30 p.m. in Atlanta, Georgia, what time is it in Unalaska, Alaska? _____ p.m.

3. What are Alaska's two time zones? _____ and _____

4. In what time zone is Colorado located? _____

5. If it is 10:00 p.m. in Anchorage, Alaska, what time is it in Mobile, Alabama? _____ a.m.

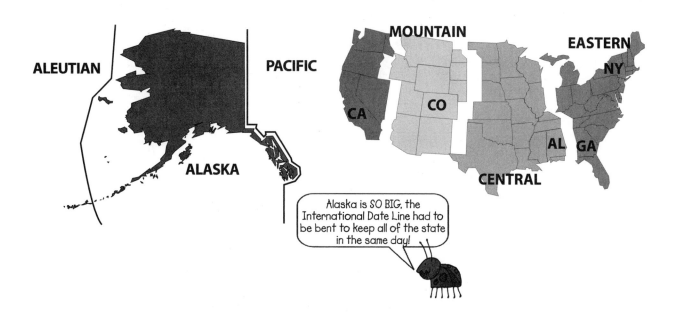

Alaska is SO BIG, the International Date Line had to be bent to keep all of the state in the same day!

Sing Like An Alaska Bird
Word Jumble

WORD BANK
Chickadee
Crane
Eagle
Gull
Loon
Magpie
Ptarmigan
Puffin
Sandpiper
Tern

Unscramble the names of these Alaska birds:

FINPUF _ _ _ _ _ _

GANMITARP _ _ _ _ _ _ _ _ _

ELGAE _ _ _ _ _

NTRE _ _ _ _

LUGL _ _ _ _

RCAEN _ _ _ _ _

NOOL _ _ _ _

PEIPRASDN _ _ _ _ _ _ _ _ _

GMAPIE _ _ _ _ _ _

ADEEKCIHC _ _ _ _ _ _ _ _ _

ANSWERS: Puffin; Ptarmigan; Eagle; Tern; Gull; Crane; Loon; Sandpiper; Magpie; Chickadee

Alaska Schools Rule!

Alaskans are among the best-educated citizens in the United States. Alaska tops the national average for high school and college graduates! Along with the many schools located throughout Alaska, students can also receive their education through the state-operated home study program.

Students in Alaska can attend one of these fine universities. **Can you figure out their names? Use the Word Bank to help you. Then, use the answers to solve the coded message at the bottom.**

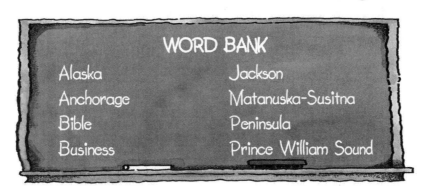

WORD BANK

Alaska | Jackson
Anchorage | Matanuska-Susitna
Bible | Peninsula
Business | Prince William Sound

1. University of __ __ __ __ __ __
                    4   7

2. Alaska __ __ __ __ __ College in Glennallen
              2

3. Alaska Pacific University in __ __ __ __ __ __ __ __ __

4. Sheldon __ __ __ __ __ __ __ College in Sitka
                        5

5. __ __ __ __ __ __ __ __ __ __ __ __ __ __ __ __ __
                                                    1
    Community College in Valdez

6. Kenai __ __ __ __ __ __ __ __ __ College
            3

7. Alaska __ __ __ __ __ __ __ __ College in Anchorage

8. __ __ __ __ __ __ __ __ __ __-__ __ __ __ __ __ __ College in
        6
    Palmer.

The coded message tells you what all college students want!

__ __ __ __ __ __ __
1 2 3 4 5 6 7

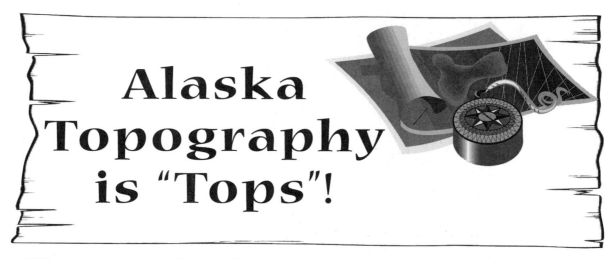

Alaska Topography is "Tops"!

When we learn about Alaska's topography, we use special words to describe it. These words describe the things that make each part of the state interesting.

Cross out every other letter below beginning with the first one to find out what each topographical term is!

1. A G W O C R K G L E: a deep, narrow passage between mountains

2. T P A E B R O M I A Q F I R U O B S Z T: ground that's been frozen for two years or more

3. L T I U Q N R D Z R O A: frozen ground that thaws just enough for wildflowers, mosses, and short grasses to grow

4. Z B P U L S E H: areas of wilderness, or areas that aren't accessible by roads

5. F G P L M A Y C W I R E X R: large mass of slow moving ice and snow that travels down a mountain or across land until it melts

6. T M Q O W U R N I T S A V I T N U S: chain or group of very high hills

7. A V I O D L W C Z A I N M O: an opening in the earth that spews molten rock

8. M C Y A P L X D M E T R Q A: large crater in a volcano

9. S F T J H O Z R W D: narrow inlet of the sea between steep cliffs

10. P T A O Y P U O M G Q R T A O P V H K Y: the detailed mapping of the features on the surface of land

ANSWERS: 1-gorge; 2-permafrost; 3-tundra; 4-bush; 5-glacier; 6-mountains; 7-volcano; 8-caldera; 9-fjord; 10-topography

Oh! Say Can You See...
The Alaska State Flag

Alaska's current state flag was adopted in 1927. It features seven gold stars on the bottom left and a single gold star. The golden stars represent Alaska's gold resources. The blue background is for Alaska's sky and state flower, the forget-me-not.

Alaska's striking flag was designed in 1926 by 13-year-old Benny Benson. His flag design was the winning entry in a competition open to all Alaska students! **Color the state flag.**

Fast Fact: The single gold star on the top right corner represents the North Star, showing Alaska's northern location.

Fast Fact: The seven stars represent the Big Dipper.

Design Your Own Diamante About Alaska!

A *diamante* is a cool diamond-shaped poem on any subject.

You can write your very own diamante poem on Alaska by following the simple line by line directions below. Give it a try!

Line 1: Write the name of the state.

Line 2: Write the names of two animals native to Alaska.

Line 3: Write the names of three cities in Alaska.

Line 4: Write the names of four of Alaska's agricultural products.

Line 5: Write the names of three Alaskan birds.

Line 6: Write the names of Alaska's state mineral and gem.

Line 7: Write the word that completes this sentence:
Alaska's nickname is the Last _____.

_____

_____ _____

_____ _____ _____

_____ _____ _____ _____

_____ _____ _____

_____ _____

_____

YOU'RE a poet!
Did you know it?

History Mystery Tour!

Alaska is bursting at the seams with history! Here are just a few of the many historical sights that you might visit.

Try your hand at locating them on the map! Then, draw a symbol for each sight on the Alaska map below.

 1. **Klondike Gold Rush National Historic Park in Skagway.** Visitors will see the historic boom town and portions of the Chilkoot and White Pass trails that led northwest through Alaska and on to the Klondike strike in the Yukon.

 2. **Iditarod Trail Sled Dog Race Headquarters and Museum in Knik** has historic memorabilia, films, and exhibits including the sleds that Susan Butcher and Joe Redington, Sr. mushed to the top of Mount McKinley.

 3. **The Alaska State Historical Library in Juneau** houses many books and documents about the history of the 49th state!

 4. **Totem Heritage Center in Ketchikan** has the largest collection of original Tsimshian, Haida, and Tlingit totems.

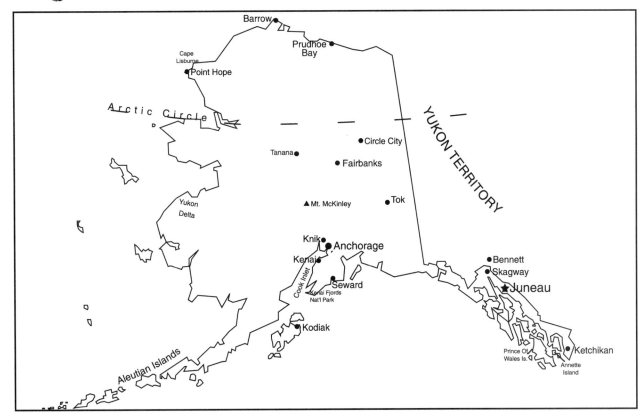

What in the World?

A hemisphere is one-half of a sphere (globe) created by the prime meridian or equator. Every place in the world is in two hemispheres (Northern or Southern and Eastern or Western). The equator is an imaginary line that runs around the world from left to right and divides the globe into the Northern Hemisphere and the Southern Hemisphere. The prime meridian is an imaginary line that runs around the world from top to bottom and divides the globe into the Eastern Hemisphere and Western Hemisphere.

Label the Northern and Southern Hemispheres.

Write E on the equator.

Is Alaska in the NORTHERN or SOUTHERN Hemisphere? (circle one)

Color the map.

Label the Eastern and Western Hemispheres.

Write PM on the prime meridian.

Is Alaska in the EASTERN or WESTERN Hemisphere? (circle one)

Color the map.

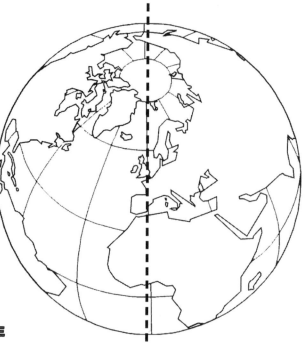

"Wild And Woolly" Life!

"Bear" with us as we "fish" around to "sea" what types of critters you will find in Alaska's wildlife preserves.

Using the words in the Word Bank, complete the names of the following wildlife preserves.

1. _ _ _ _ _ _ National Wildlife Refuge, Fairbanks

2. American _ _ _ _ _ _ _ _ _ Foundation, Haines

3. Beluga _ _ _ _ _ Lookout, Kenai

4. Deer Mountain Tribal _ _ _ _ _ _ _ _, Ketchikan

5. Alaska _ _ _ _ _ _ _ Center, Seward

6. Pack _ _ _ _ Creek Observatory, Admiralty Island

7. _ _ _ _ _ _ _ _ Research Station, Cantwell

8. _ _ _ _ _ _ Islands State Game Sanctuary

WORD BANK

Arctic	Reindeer
Bald Eagle	Sealife
Bear	Walrus
Hatchery	Whale

Please Come to Alaska!
The Scenery Is Great!

You have a friend named Kelly who lives in Virginia, one of the Lower 48 states. Her family is thinking of moving to Alaska because they love the great outdoors. Kelly wants to be a mountaineering guide, and Alaska is the place for guiding climbers up, up, up those magnificent mountains!

Kelly has researched Alaska's topography and found there are 39 mountain ranges. The highest peak in all of North America is Mount McKinley, which is also called Denali. She has discovered that every year about 1,000 climbers try to reach the top of Mount McKinley. And of course, all those adventurous climbers are going to need a great mountain climbing guide!

Kelly has read about some of the legendary Mount McKinley "firsts." In 1913, Hudson Stuck's expedition reaches the top of the South Peak—the highest peak of all. In 1932, bush pilot Joe Crosson makes the first glacial landing on Muldrow Glacier. In 1979 mushers Joe Redington, Sr. and Susan Butcher mush to the top! Kelly dreams that someday she'll have a Mount McKinley "first" of her very own!

Gold! The Rush Is On!

The first Alaskan gold strike struck in 1872 near **Sitka**! The gold rush was on! In 1880, Joe Juneau and Dick Harris struck it rich near present-day **Juneau**. Native Tlingit guides led them to rich gold deposits along the Gastineau Channel. Other big strikes occurred in **Circle City** in 1893, **Nome** in 1898, and **Fairbanks** in 1902.

Thousands of gold seekers were on their way to "get rich quick!" Fortune hunters stampeded the regions, set up tents, and started digging and panning. The "tent cities" of Juneau, **Douglas**, and **Treadwell** boomed into "boom towns."

Now it's your turn! Go digging for the answers to this puzzle. To "strike it rich," fill in all the locations of the big gold strikes and boom towns. They're buried deep in the story above!

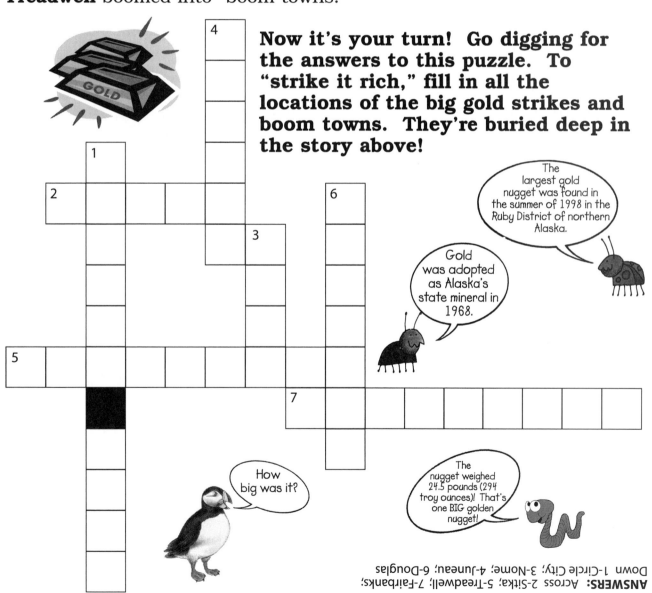

The largest gold nugget was found in the summer of 1998 in the Ruby District of northern Alaska.

Gold was adopted as Alaska's state mineral in 1968.

How big was it?

The nugget weighed 24.5 pounds (294 troy ounces)! That's one BIG golden nugget!

Alaska Rules!

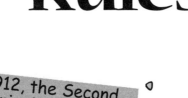

The Organic Act of 1884 gave Alaska its first civil government, a territorial legislature with limited powers.

In 1912, the Second Organic Act declared Alaska a territory.

Use the code to complete the sentences.

A	B	C	D	E	F	G	H	I	J	K	L	M	N	O	P
1	2	3	4	5	6	7	8	9	10	11	12	13	14	15	16

Q	R	S	T	U	V	W	X	Y	Z
17	18	19	20	21	22	23	24	25	26

1. State rules are called __ __ __ __.
          12 1 23 19

   In 1959, Alaska became the 49th state.

2. Laws are made in our state __ __ __ __ __ __ __.
          3 1 16 9 20 15 12

3. The leader of our state is the __ __ __ __ __ __ __ __.
          7 15 22 5 18 14 15 18

4. We live in the state of __ __ __ __ __ __.
          1 12 1 19 11 1

   In 1971, the Alaska Native Claims Settlement Act granted title to 40 million acres (16 million hectares) of land and provided $900 million in payment.

5. The capital of our state is __ __ __ __ __ __.
          10 21 14 5 1 21

A L A S K A ! ! !

Buzzing Around Alaska!

Write the answers to the questions below. To get to the beehive, follow a path through the maze.

1. Wrangell-_____ _____ National Park and Preserve is the largest U.S. national park.
2. _____ is on top of the world. It's the northernmost community in the United States.
3. The magnificent Holy Assumption Russian Orthodox Church is located in _____.
4. _____ is the largest glacier in North America!
5. Alaska has the world's longest chain of active volcanoes. They are part of the Pacific Ocean's _____ _____ _____!
6. _____ National Historic Park is the site of the Tlingits' final battle of resistance against the Russians in 1804.
7. The _____ _____ is the name for the U.S. mainland.
8. The _____ Islands are the southwestern part of Alaska. The Panhandle is the southeastern part of Alaska.
9. The _____ Sea flows between Alaska and Russia.
10. _____ borders Alaska on the east.

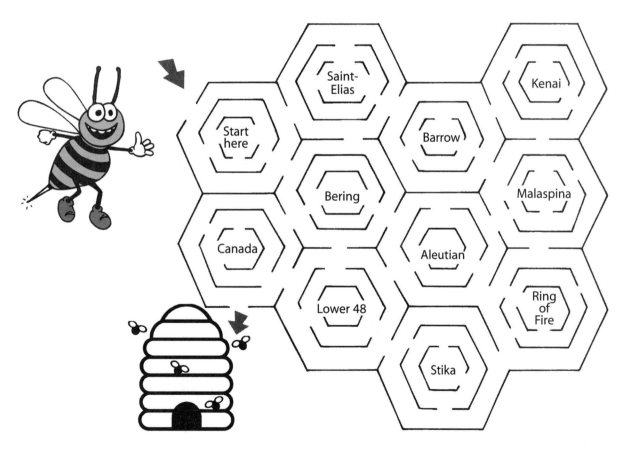

Alaska Through the Years!

Many great things have happened in Alaska throughout its history. Chronicle the following important Alaska events by solving math problems to find out the years in which they happened.

1. Czar Peter the Great of Russia sends Vitus Bering to explore North Pacific.

   $6÷6=$ $3+4=$ $4-2=$ $2+3=$

2. On second expedition, Bering and Chirikov sight Alaska.

   $9÷9=$ $9-2=$ $2x2=$ $8-7=$

3. Russians establish settlement on Kodiak Island.

   $4-3=$ $2+5=$ $4x2=$ $8-4=$

4. Trade charter is granted to Russian-American Company.

   $2-1=$ $1+6=$ $10-1=$ $3x3=$

5. William Henry Seward negotiates purchase of Alaska from Russia; U.S. buys Alaska for $7.2 million.

   $8-7=$ $4x2=$ $3x2=$ $1+6=$

6. Alaska becomes 49th state.

   $6-5=$ $3x3=$ $9-4=$ $2+7=$

7. The Good Friday earthquake demolishes Anchorage and Valdez, killing 131 people.

   $6÷6=$ $3+6=$ $4+2=$ $2+2=$

8. Alaska Native Claims Settlement Act grants title to 40 million acres (16 million hectares) of land and provides $900 million in payment.

   $1+0=$ $2+7=$ $4+3=$ $7-6=$

9. Alaska National Interest Lands Conservation Act transfers 53.7 million acres (21.7 million hectares) to national wildlife refuge system.

   $6-5=$ $1+8=$ $2x4=$ $9-9=$

10. Worst oil spill in U.S. history occurs as the Exxon Valdez runs aground in Prince William Sound.

    $4÷4=$ $5+4=$ $6+2=$ $2+7=$

ANSWERS: 1-1725; 2-1741; 3-1784; 4-1799; 5-1867; 6-1959; 7-1964; 8-1971; 9-1980; 10-1989

What Did We Do Before Money?

In early Alaska, there were no banks. However, people still wanted to barter, trade, or otherwise "purchase" goods from each other. In the barter system, people swapped goods or services. Later, banks came into existence, and people began to use money to buy goods. However, they also still bartered when they had no money to spend.

Today, some Alaska Natives live in the cities using modern-day conveniences and money-exchanging systems like banks. But, many Alaska Natives still live a subsistence life, using traditional methods to hunt, gather, and fish—just like their ancestors did!

Place a star in the box below the systems used today.

Rhymin' Riddles

1. I am a northwestern state, the most northern of all;
   With rivers, lakes, and mountains that stand tall!

   What am I? _____

2. We came to this land from across the sea in search of furs;
   Bering and Chirikov were the first of our explorers.

   Who are we? _____

3. We lived in Alaska before the explorers did roam;
   The Aleutian Islands in the Pacific Ocean were our home.

   Who are we? _____

4. Of these we have lots, and they're sure to blow!
   Do you know the name of one active volcano?

   What am I? _____

 # Map Symbols

Make up symbols for these names and draw them in the space provided on the right.

mountain	
river	
lake	
glacier	
volcano	
airport	
capital	
oil	
mining	

Alaska Goodies!

Match the name of each crop or product from Alaska with the picture of that item.

Fisheries employ more Alaskans than any other private industry

Most of Alaska's farm products come from the fertile Matanuska-Susitna Valley north of Anchorage.

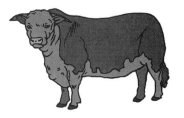

Milk

Beef cattle

Chickens

Strawberries

Seafood

Reindeer

Hay

The total annual harvest of salmon including pink, chinook, chum, sockeye, coho, and pollock is more than 1 billion fish! That many fish laid end to end would wrap around the world 16 times!

Alaska's seafood "catch of the day" leads the nation! The annual seafood harvest is worth more than $1.8 billion.

Historical Alaska Women World Wonders!

Alaska has been the home of many brave and influential women. Can you match these women with their historic accomplishments?

1. Fran Ulmer

2. Della "Puyuk" Keats

3. Susan Butcher

4. Celia Hunter

5. Barbara Washburn

6. Libby Riddles

7. Naomi Uemura

8. Dorothy Page

9. Nora M. Dauenhauer

10. Kate Carmack

A. Japanese climber; made the first "solo" ascent to Mount McKinley's summit

B. Four-time winner of Iditarod; first person ever to win three Iditarod races in a row

C. Tagish Tlingit who helped discover the Klondike gold

D. Ferried U.S. military airplanes to bases during World War II; active in efforts to protect Alaska's environment; president of The Wilderness Society, national environmental organization

E. Inuit healer; combined modern medicine with ancient skills as tribal doctor and midwife

F. In 1985, became first woman to win the Iditarod

G. First woman to reach the top of Mount McKinley; husband climbed with her to the top

H. Historian, who along with musher Joe Redington, Sr. organized the Iditarod Trail Sled Dog Race

I. Author whose love of her native language led her to collect, translate, and preserve stories passed down by word of mouth through generations of Tlingits

J. Juneau mayor; state senator; as lieutenant governor, became first woman elected to a statewide office

ANSWERS: 1-J; 2-E; 3-B; 4-D; 5-G; 6-F; 7-A; 8-H; 9-I; 10-C

Producers and Consumers

Producers (sellers) make goods or provide services. Ralph, a 4th grade student in Anchorage, is a consumer because he wants to buy a new wheel for his bicycle. Other products and services from Alaska that consumers can buy include:

Computer equipment
Paper products
Electrical machinery
Mountaineering guide
Tour Guide

In 1968, oil was discovered in Prudhoe Bay. It's the largest oil field in North America and makes up 25 percent of known oil deposits in the United States! The oil discovered in Prudhoe Bay led to the building of the Trans-Alaska pipeline.

Complete these sentences.

Without oil for gasoline, I couldn't

_____

_____

Without computer equipment, I couldn't

_____

_____

Without a mountaineering guide, I couldn't

_____

_____

Without paper products, I couldn't

_____

_____

Alaska Word Wheel!

Use the Word Wheel of Alaska names to complete the sentences below.

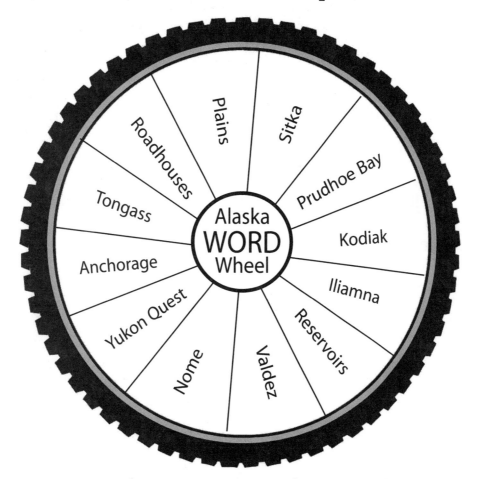

1. _____ is the transportation and commercial center for northwestern Alaska.

2. _____ has the highest population of all Alaskan cities.

3. Oil was discovered in _____ _____ in 1968.

4. The largest Alaskan island is _____.

5. _____ is the largest city in area of Alaskan cities.

6. The Iditarod and the _____ _____ are two of the longest sled dog races in the world!

7. _____ is the largest natural freshwater lake in Alaska.

8. _____ are an important part of Alaska's history. They offered bed and board at a modest price for travelers on Alaska's early trails. A few survive to this day!

9. _____ is the largest national forest in the United States.

10. The Trans-Alaska Pipeline carries up to 88,000 barrels of oil per hour over its 800-mile route to _____.

What A Way To Go!

Alaska has about 13,000 miles (20,921 kilometers) of roadways, including roads in national parks and forests. Some of the highways in Alaska are speedy six-lane paved freeways! Some highways are covered in gravel and some are one-lane dirt roads! Only about 30 percent of the roads in Alaska's highway system are paved.

Using the map below to help you, write down the direction you'd travel and the highway you'd take in order to get from:

1. Anchorage to Seward = _____

2. Prudhoe Bay to Fairbanks = _____

3. Fairbanks to Circle City= _____

4. Skagway to Bennett = _____

5. Tok to Fairbanks = _____

Create Your Own Alaska State Quarter!

Look at the change in your pocket. You might notice that one of the coins has changed. The United States is minting new quarters, one for each of the 50 states. Each quarter has a design on it that says something special about one particular state. The Alaska quarter will be in cash registers and piggy banks everywhere after it's released in 2008.

What if you had designed the Alaska quarter? Draw a picture of how you would like the Alaska quarter to look. Make sure you include things that are special about Alaska.

Alaska Law Comes In Many Flavors!

For each of these people, write down the kind(s) of law used to decide whether their actions are legal or illegal.

1. Bank robber _____
2. Business person _____
3. State park ranger _____
4. Alaskans _____
5. Doctor _____
6. Real estate agent _____
7. Corporate president _____
8. Ship owner _____
9. Diplomat _____
10. Soldier _____

Medical Law

International Law

Military Law

Maritime Law

Antitrust Law

Commercial Law

Criminal Law

State Law

Environmental Law

Property Law

Mixed-Up States!

Color each of Alaska's "Lower 48" Pacific state neighbors on the map below. Alaska also has some special Canadian neighbors—the Yukon Territory and British Columbia.

ALASKA

YUKON

Color me Yukon Gold!

Color me Canadian red!

BRITISH COLUMBIA

Color me all the colors of the Aurora Borealis

Color me Pacific blue!

Color me evergreen!

WA

OR

Color me California orange!

CA

Ahoy There, Matey!

Many of Alaska's coastal towns are most easily reached by water instead of roads. Ferry transportation is provided by the Alaska Marine Highway and includes two state ferry systems called Inside Passage/Southeast and Southcentral/Southwest.

When you're on board any kind of boat, you have to use special terms to talk about directions. Label the ship below with these terms:

bow: front of the ship
stern: back of the ship
fore: towards the bow
aft: towards the stern
port: left as you face the bow
starboard: right as you face the bow

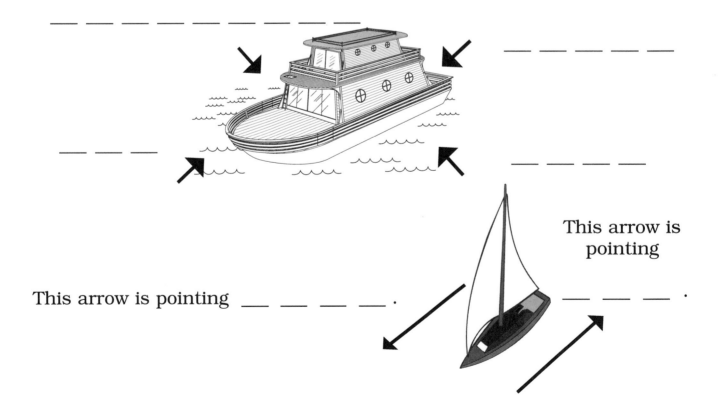

This arrow is pointing __ __ __ __ .

This arrow is pointing __ __ __ __ .

Alaska Politics As Usual!

Our elected government officials decide how much money is going to be spent on schools, roads, public parks, and libraries. It's very important for the citizens of Alaska to understand what's going on in their government, and how it will affect them.

Alaska's government has three branches, the Executive, Legislative, and Judicial. Under the state constitution, "redistricting" is done every 10 years, following the federal census.

On the lines provided, write down a question for each of the answers below. A hint follows each answer.

1. Question: _____
   Answer: A draft of a law presented for review.
   (Short for William!)

2. Question: _____
   Answer: The right to vote.
   (Don't make us suffer!)

3. Question: _____
   Answer: The ability to forbid a bill or law from being passed.
   (Just say no!)

4. Question: _____
   Answer: The fundamental law of the United States that was framed in 1787 and put into effect in 1789.
   (Alaska has one too!)

5. Question: _____
   Answer: An amendment.
   (It's not something subtracted from #4!)

ANSWERS: (may vary slightly) 1-What is a bill? 2-What is suffrage? 3-What is a veto? 4-What is the Constitution? 5-What is an addition to the Constitution called?

What Shall I Be When I Grow Up?

Here are just a few of the jobs that kept early Alaskans busy.

Lawyer	Carpenter	Baker
Farmer	Weaver	Guide
Woodcarver	Barber	Gaoler (jailer)
Judge	Gardener	Fisherman
Housekeeper	Lumberjack	Doctor
Silversmith	Printer	Missionary
Politician	Cook	Milliner (hatmaker)
Dairyman	Musician	Soldier
Wheelwright	Bookbinder	Hunter
Teacher	Laundress	Blacksmith
Servant	Jeweler	Sailor
Cabinetmaker	Innkeeper	Trapper
Hunter	Stablehand	Gunsmith
Whaler	Tailor	Prospector
Cooper (barrelmaker)	Minister	Tanner

You are a young settler trying to decide what you want to be when you grow up.

Choose a career and next to it write a description of what you think you would do each day as a:

Write your career choice here!
_____

_____
_____
_____

Write your career choice here!
_____

_____
_____
_____

Write your career choice here!
_____

_____
_____
_____

Write your career choice here!
_____

_____
_____
_____

Governor of Alaska!

The governor is the leader of the state.

You've been assigned to write a biography of the governor of Alaska.

Before you can start your book, you need to jot down some notes in your trusty computer. Fill in the necessary information in the spaces provided on the dossier!

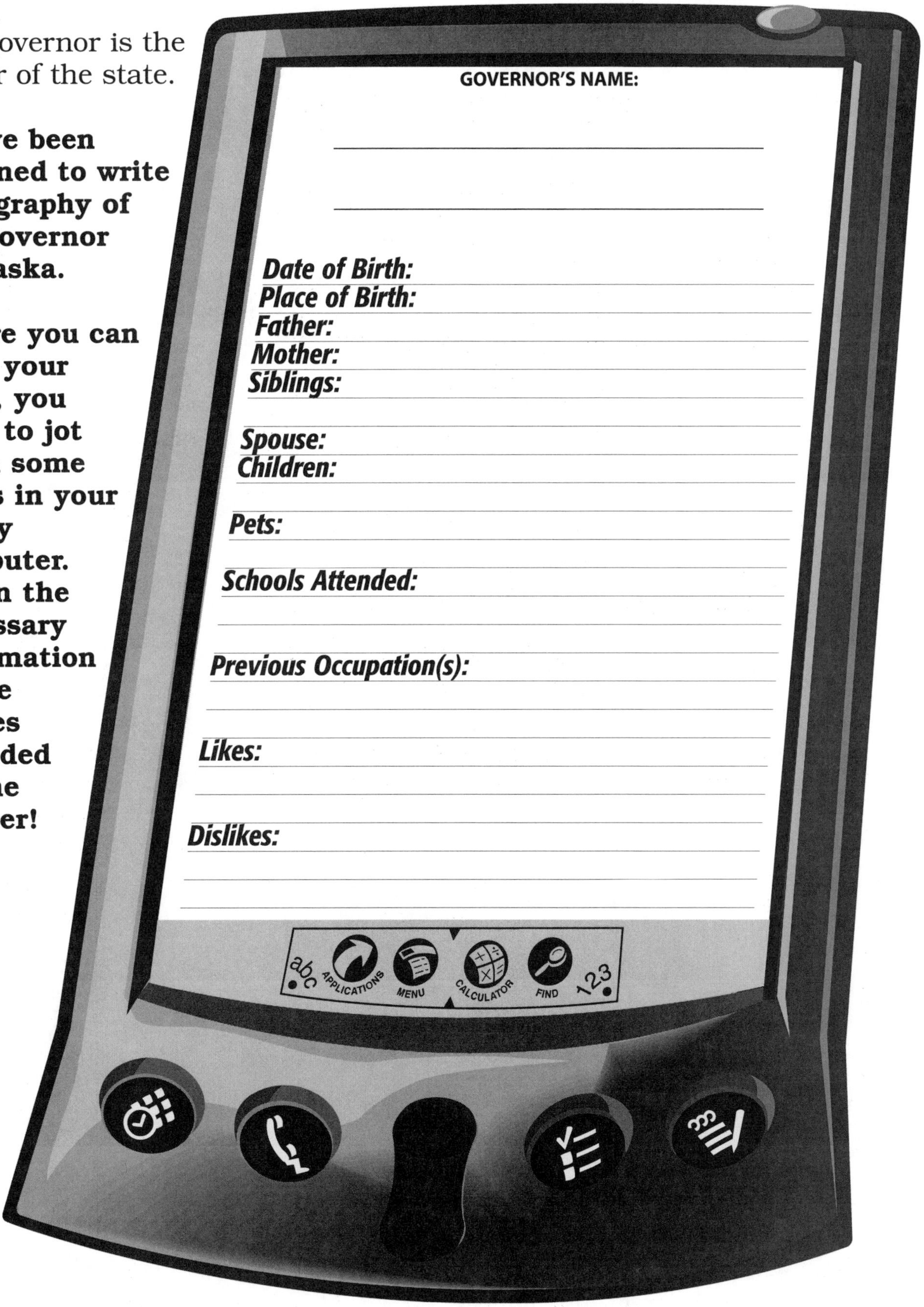

GOVERNOR'S NAME:

_____

_____

Date of Birth: _____

Place of Birth: _____

Father: _____

Mother: _____

Siblings: _____

_____

Spouse: _____

Children: _____

_____

Pets: _____

_____

Schools Attended: _____

_____

_____

Previous Occupation(s): _____

_____

_____

Likes: _____

_____

_____

Dislikes: _____

_____

_____

abc • APPLICATIONS • MENU • CALCULATOR • FIND • 123

The ORIGINAL Alaska Natives!

What kinds of things did early Alaska Natives use in their everyday life? Alaska's earliest residents were the Eskimo, Indian, and Aleut peoples. Each ethnic group lived in its own special part of Alaska and each had a distinctive culture. Today, many Alaska Natives live a subsistence life—just as their ancient ancestors did!

What kinds of things did Native Americans use in their everyday life? For each of the things shown, circle YES if Native Americans did use it, or NO if they didn't.

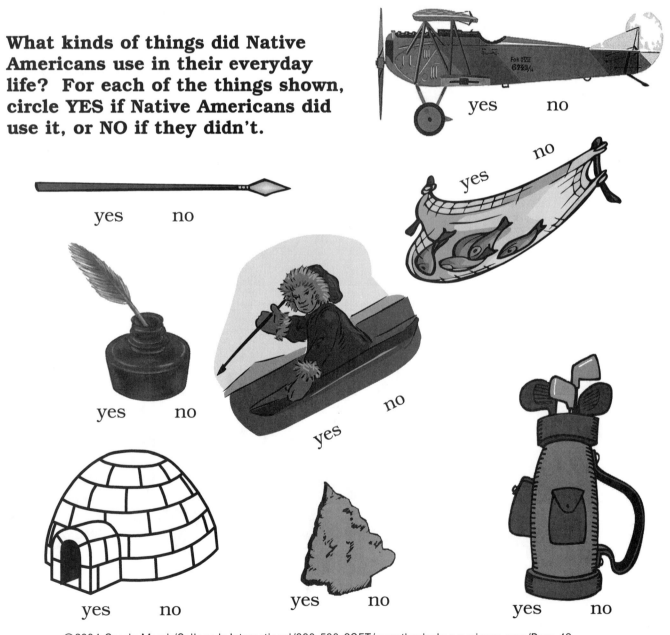

yes   no

yes   no

yes   no

yes   no

yes   no

yes   no

yes   no

yes   no

States All Around Code-Buster!

Decipher the code and write in the names of the states that border Alaska.

A B C D E F G H I J K L M N O P Q R

S T U V W X Y Z

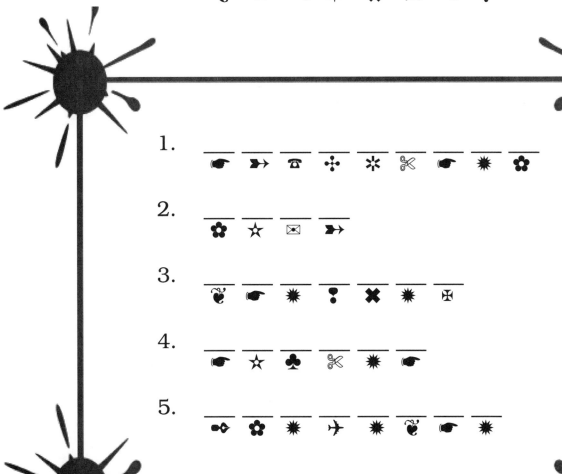

1. _____

2. _____

3. _____

4. _____

5. _____

Unique Alaska Place Names!

Can you figure out the compound words that make up the names of these Alaska places?

Buckland   _____   _____

Goodhope   _____   _____

Fairbanks   _____   _____

Southeast   _____   _____

Fairweather   _____   _____

Upright   _____   _____

Blackburn   _____   _____

Inland   _____   _____

Portland   _____   _____

Sleetmute   _____   _____

Sunshine   _____   _____

Tanacross   _____   _____

Totson   _____   _____

Northeast   _____   _____

Witherspoon   _____   _____

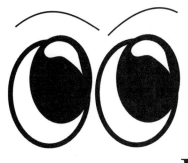

Looking For a Home In The Last Frontier!

Starting with the first, circle every other letter to find out which animal is looking for a home in Alaska!

1. Alaska has lots of bears! Lots of different kinds of bears! Black bears, brown bears, grizzly bears, and _ _ _ _ _ bears!
   (P Q O I L P A V R)

2. A large group of Alaskan brown or _ _ _ _ _ _ _ bears lives on Kodiak Island. This is the largest carnivorous land mammal in the world.
   (K U O C D L I S A B K)

3. Herds of _ _ _ _ _ _ _ _ inhabit the Arctic Slope and the Brooks Range.
   (C E A H R O I X B M O Y U)

4. Big, shaggy _ _ _ _ _-_ _ _ _ live on Nunivak Island.
   (M P U T S R K-F O D X F E L N)

5. Many of Alaska's mountain ranges have herds of mountain _ _ _ _ _ _ and long-haired _ _ _ _ sheep.
   (G E O C A H T P S / D W A K L C L)

6. Chilkat Bald Eagle Preserve near Haines has the largest gathering of _ _ _ _ _ _ _ _ _ _ _ in the world!
   (B R A C L R D   E P A H G K L R E C S)

ANSWERS: 1-polar; 2-Kodiak; 3-caribou; 4-musk-oxen; 5-goats, Dall; 6-bald eagles

I Love Alaska, Weather Or Not!

Alaska's different geographical features create many different climates throughout the state. Alaska's interior experiences colder winters and warmer summers. The Arctic region is colder, while southern Alaska has milder temperatures.

Alaska's highest temperature was 100°F (38°C), at Fort Yukon, on June 27, 1915. The coldest temperature was a brisk -80°F (-62°C) at Prospect Creek Camp on January 23, 1971.

During the Gold Rush of 1898, an avalanche on Chilkoot Trail buries hundreds of stampeders heading for the Yukon. Seventy prospectors die. Shorty Fisher's sled dog, Jack, survives for eight days under the snowslide and lives to mush again!

The 1964 Good Friday earthquake demolishes Anchorage and Valdez, killing 131 people. The earthquake creates tidal waves as far south as California. It's the strongest earthquake to strike North America ever and would measure 9.2 on today's Richter scale!

On the thermometer gauges below, color the mercury red (°F) to show the hottest temperature ever recorded in Alaska. Color the mercury blue (°F) to show the coldest temperature ever recorded in Alaska.

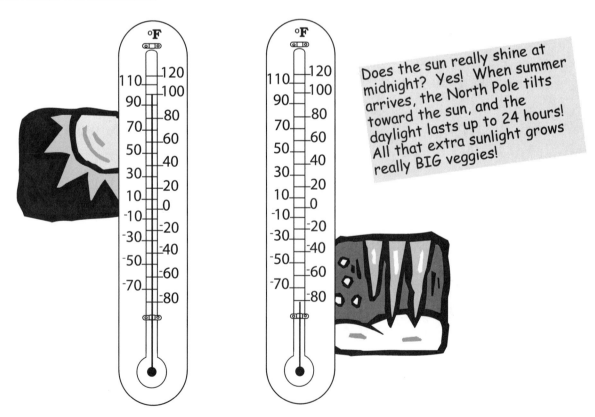

Does the sun really shine at midnight? Yes! When summer arrives, the North Pole tilts toward the sun, and the daylight lasts up to 24 hours! All that extra sunlight grows really BIG veggies!

The Scenic Route

Imagine that you've planned an exciting exploratory expedition around Alaska for your classmates. You've chosen some cities and other places to take your friends.

Circle these sites and cities on the map below, then number them in the order you would visit if you were traveling north to south through the state:

___ Alaska State Library in Anchorage
___ Kenai Fjords National Park
___ Beluga Whale Lookout in Kenai
___ Mount McKinley
___ Whalebone arch in Barrow
___ Alutiiq Museum in Kodiak
___ Tanana Mission
___ Alaska Sealife Center in Seward

Barrow
Prudhoe Bay
Cape Lisburne
Point Hope
Arctic Circle
YUKON TERRITORY
Circle City
Tanana
Fairbanks
Yukon Delta
▲ Mt. McKinley
Tok
Knik
Anchorage
Kenai
Bennett
Skagway
★ Juneau
Cook Inlet
Seward
Kenai Fjords Nat'l Park
N NE NW W E SW SE S
Kodiak
Aleutian Islands
Prince Of Wales Is.
Ketchikan
Annette Island

ANSWERS WILL APPEAR IN THIS ORDER: 4;7;5;3;1;8;2;6

Key to a Map!

A map key, also called a map legend, shows symbols which represent different things on a map.

Match each word with a symbol for things found in the state of Alaska.

airport (Merrill Field)

church (Cathedral of St. Michael)

mountains (Mount McKinley)

railroad (Alaska Railroad)

river (Yukon)

road (Alcan)

school (University of Alaska)

state capital (Juneau)

battle site (Attu and Kiska islands)

bird sanctuary (Alaska Raptor Rehabilitation Center)

BROTHER, CAN YOU SPARE A DIME?

After the collapse of the stock market on Wall Street in 1929, the United States plunged headfirst into the Great Depression. It was the worst economic crisis America had ever known. Banks closed and businesses crashed...there was financial ruin everywhere.

Although Alaska was not a state in 1929, it was a U.S. territory affected by the stock market crash of 1929! During the Great Depression, Alaska's population grew! Many Americans came from the Lower 48 looking for new opportunities! The federal government wanted to help these families begin a new life. Two hundred farm families from the Midwestern states were resettled in Alaska's fertile Matanuska Valley.

Our President Helps

While the nation was in the midst of the Depression, Franklin Delano Roosevelt became president. With America on the brink of economic devastation, the federal government stepped forward and hired unemployed people to build parks, bridges, and roads. With this help, and other government assistance, the country began to slowly, and painfully, pull out of the Great Depression. Within the first 100 days of his office, Roosevelt enacted a number of policies to help minimize the suffering of the nation's many unemployed workers. These programs were known as the NEW DEAL. The jobs helped families support themselves and improved the country's infrastructure.

Put an X next to the jobs that were part of Roosevelt's New Deal.

1. computer programmer _____

2. bridge builder _____

3. fashion model _____

4. park builder _____

5. interior designer _____

6. hospital builder _____

7. school builder _____

8. website designer _____

ANSWERS: 2 4 6 7

Alaska Newcomers!

    People have come to Alaska from the Lower 48 states and many other countries! As time goes by, Alaska's population grows more diverse. This means that people of different races and from different cultures and ethnic backgrounds have moved to Alaska.

    In the past, many immigrants have come to Alaska from Canada, Scandinavia, Japan, and the Philippines. More recently, people have migrated to Alaska from South Korea, Taiwan, other Asian countries, and Hispanic countries such as Mexico. Only a certain number of immigrants are allowed to move to America each year. Many of these immigrants eventually become U.S. citizens.

Read the statement and decide if it's a fact or an opinion. Write your answer on the line.

1. Many of Alaska's early immigrants came from Canada.
   _____

2. Lots of immigrants speak a language other than English.
   _____

3. The clothing immigrants wear is very interesting.
   _____

4. Immigrants from Scandinavia have a neat accent when they speak. _____

5. Many immigrants will become United States citizens.
   _____

6. People have immigrated to Alaska from nearly every country in the world. _____

An immigrant is a person who migrates to another country in hopes of a better life.

ANSWERS: 1-Fact; 2-Fact; 3-Opinion; 4-Opinion; 5-Fact; 6-Fact

A Day In The Life Of A "Sourdough"

Pretend you are a Sourdough prospecting for gold in the days of early Alaska. You keep a diary of what you do each day. Write in the "diary" what you might have done on a long, hot summer day in July 1898!

This Old House!

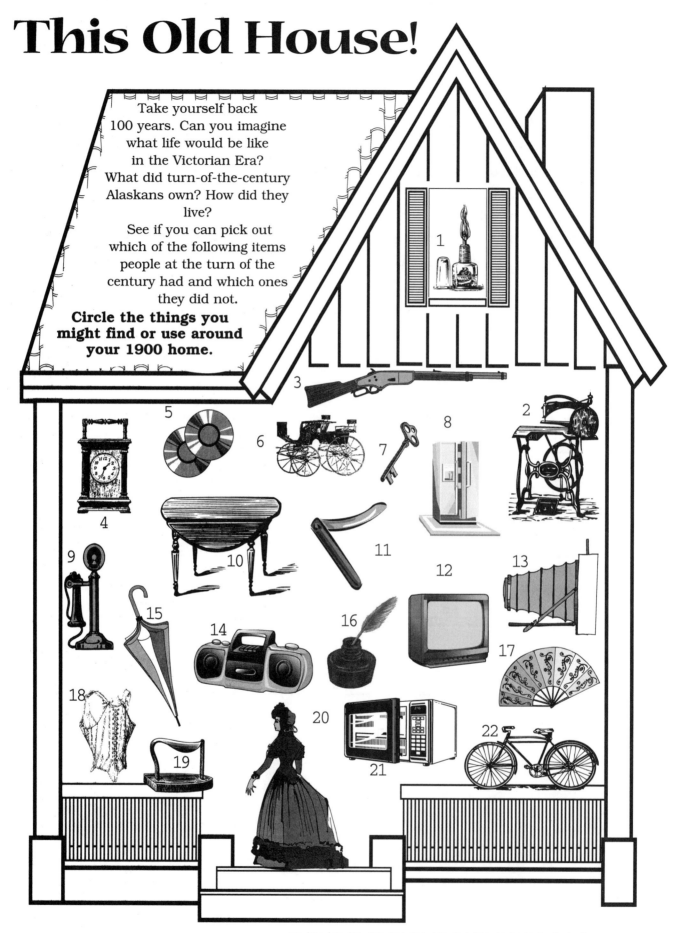

Take yourself back 100 years. Can you imagine what life would be like in the Victorian Era? What did turn-of-the-century Alaskans own? How did they live?

See if you can pick out which of the following items people at the turn of the century had and which ones they did not.

Circle the things you might find or use around your 1900 home.

Home, Sweet Home!

Alaska has been home to many different authors, poets, and other writers. Here are just a few. See if you can locate their hometowns on the map of Alaska below! Write the number of each author near the town where he or she lived. Some towns may be used twice.

1. Margaret G. Mielke—author, poet, and poetry editor for *Anchorage Times*; in 1963, she was chosen to be the first Poet Laureate of Alaska (home—large city on the coast in Cook Inlet)

2. Margaret E. Murie—one of Alaska's best-loved writers and most passionate conservationists; wrote *Two in the Far North* and *Wapiti Wilderness*; co-founder of the Arctic Wildlife Range in 1960 with husband Olaus Murie (home—large city northeast of Mount McKinley)

3. Rex Beach—came to Alaska to dig for gold; author; wrote stories about wild Alaskan lands filled with danger, danger, danger—and the courageous men and women who lived and died on the wild frontier (frontier home was wild and woolly and the place for gold!)

4. Ann Fox Chandonnet—poet, author, journalist, founding member of the Literary Artists Guild; works include *Poems for my Aleut-Athabascan Son* and *Ptarmigan Valley* (home—large city on the coast in Cook Inlet)

5. John Griffith London, better known as Jack London—author; famous for stories of adventure; works include *The Call of the Wild*, (frontier home was wild and woolly and the place for gold!)

6. Howard Rock—founder of The Tundra Times newspaper, (home—coastal city north of Arctic Circle southwest of Cape Lisburne)

ANSWERS: 1-Anchorage; 2-Fairbanks; 3-Yukon; 4-Anchorage; 5-Yukon; 6-Point Hope

Alaska Spelling Bee!

Good spelling is a good habit. Study the words on the left side of the page. Then fold the page in half and "take a spelling test" on the right side. Have a buddy read the words aloud to you. When finished, unfold the page and check your spelling. Keep your score. GOOD LUCK.

Each word is worth 5 points.

Alaska	_____
aurora borealis	_____
Aleutian Islands	_____
blubber	_____
Chilkoot Trail	_____
Denali	_____
eagles	_____
glaciers	_____
greenhorns	_____
grizzly bears	_____
Iditarod	_____
Juneau	_____
Klondike	_____
moose	_____
mush	_____
peninsula	_____
reindeer	_____
snow	_____
sourdoughs	_____
volcanoes	_____

A perfect score is 100! How many did you get right?

Naturally Alaska!

Fill in the bubblegram with some Alaska crops and natural resources. Use the letter clues to help you.

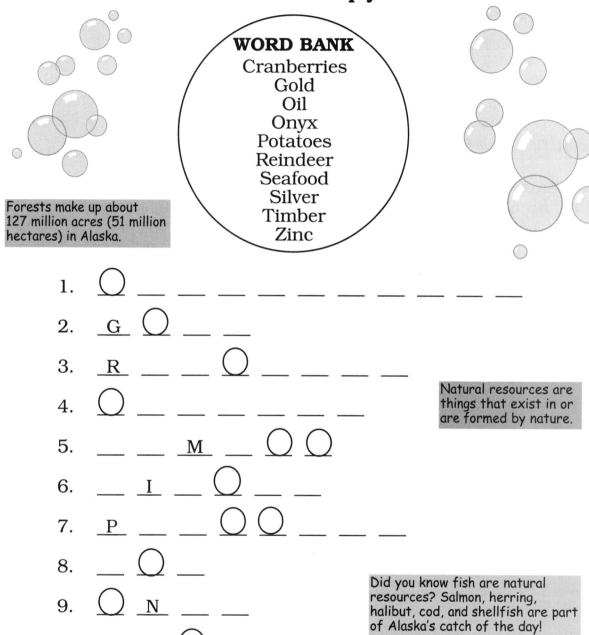

WORD BANK
Cranberries
Gold
Oil
Onyx
Potatoes
Reindeer
Seafood
Silver
Timber
Zinc

Forests make up about 127 million acres (51 million hectares) in Alaska.

Natural resources are things that exist in or are formed by nature.

1. ◯ _ _ _ _ _ _ _ _ _ _

2. G ◯ _ _

3. R _ _ ◯ _ _ _ _

4. ◯ _ _ _ _ _ _ _

5. _ _ M _ ◯ ◯

6. _ I _ ◯ _ _

7. P _ _ ◯ ◯ _ _ _

8. _ ◯ _

9. ◯ N _ _

10. _ _ ◯ C

Did you know fish are natural resources? Salmon, herring, halibut, cod, and shellfish are part of Alaska's catch of the day!

Now unscramble the "bubble" letters to find out the mystery word! HINT: What is one way we can help to save our environment?

_ _ _ _ _ _ _ _ _ _ _ _

ANSWERS: 1-cranberries; 2-gold; 3-reindeer; 4-seafood; 5-timber; 6-silver; 7-potatoes; 8-oil; 9-onyx; 10-zinc
MYSTERY WORD: conservation

Have You Heard?

   Most Alaska Natives speak English as well as their own language. Yupik, Central Yupik, Siberian Yupik, and Inupiaq are Eskimo languages that are widely spoken across western and northern Alaska. Of the more than 20 Native American languages spoken in Alaska, 15 are at risk of becoming extinct—of being heard no more.

Put the names of these "endangered" languages in alphabetical order by numbering them 1 to 15.

_____ Han

_____ Haida

_____ Eyak

_____ Tanana

_____ Tlingit

_____ Dena'ina

_____ Ahtna

_____ Ingalik

_____ Holikachuk

_____ Tsimshian

_____ Koyukon

_____ Upper Kuskokwim

_____ Upper Tanana

_____ Kutchin

_____ Aleut

ANSWERS: will appear in this order: 6; 5; 4; 11; 12; 3; 1; 8; 7; 13; 9; 14; 15; 10; 2

What a Great Idea!

Alaska
Alaska Film Office
Cable television
Donald Simpson
Wien Alaska Airlines

Fast Facts:
- Chester and Helen Seveck performed traditional Eskimo dances during early years of the Eskimo-Indian Olympics.
- The Alaska Film Office is a division of the Office of Tourism and works to make money from filmmaking in Alaska.
- Wien Alaska Airline pilots were sometimes called "Wienie birds."

1. Chester and Helen Seveck promoted _ _ _ _ _ _ for Wien Alaska Airlines through the United States and Japan for 20 years.

2. _ _ _ _ _ _ _ _ _ _ _ _ _ _ was a film producer whose hit movies include *Flashdance, Top Gun,* and *Beverly Hills Cop.*

3. The _ _ _ _ _ _ _ _ _ _ _ _ _ _ _ _ _ was formed in 1982 to promote Alaska as a great place to make films!

4. Noel Wien, a legendary bush pilot with an excellent sense of direction, formed _ _ _ _ _ _ _ _ _ _ _ _ _ _ _ _ _ _ _ with his brother Ralph.

5. Leroy Parsons invented _ _ _ _ _ _ _ _ _ _ _ _ _ _ _ _. He installed Alaska's first cable system and allowed residents in some areas to watch TV for the first time ever!

Famous Alaska People Scavenger Hunt!

Here is a list of some of the famous people associated with our state. Go on a scavenger hunt to see if you can "capture" a fact about each one. Use an encyclopedia, almanac, or other resource you might need. Happy hunting!

Austin Lathrop _____

Jay S. Hammond _____

B. Frank Heintzleman _____

Dove Kull _____

William "Willie" Hensley _____

Charles E. Bunnell _____

Chief Kowee _____

Sydney Lawrence _____

Genie Chance _____

John Muir _____

William A. Egan _____

Betzi Woodman _____

Jennie Alexander _____

Ernest Gruening _____

Wilma Knox _____

Walter J. Hickel _____

Georg Steller _____

Joe Juneau _____

Lisa Rudd _____

Carl Ben Eielson _____

The Lights Are On!

Use the words from the Word Bank to fill in the blanks in these Alaska legends. Some may be used more than once.

WORD BANK
Aurora borealis
Earth's
Electrons
Fall
Hundreds
Light shows
Magnetic field
Protons
Spring

Colors of red and green, blue and purple blaze through the night skies in northern latitudes! Shimmering lights form patterns that range from simple arcs to drapery-like forms.

The _ _ _ _ _ _ _ _ _ _ _ _ _ _ _, or northern lights, most often shimmer in the _ _ _ _ _ _ and _ _ _ _ because of _ _ _ _ _' _ position in relation to the sun—it tilts! Light shows may occur on dark, winter nights, too!

Northern lights are caused by _ _ _ _ _ _ _ _ _ and _ _ _ _ _ _ _ _ that shoot out from the sun. These charged particles drift around in space and are pulled into the Earth's _ _ _ _ _ _ _ _ _ _ _ _ _ _. They strike gas particles in the atmosphere and turn on the northern lights!

_ _ _ _ _ _ _ _ _ _ _ _ _ can occur as low as 40 miles (64 kilometers) above the Earth's surface and extend for _ _ _ _ _ _ _ _ of miles into space! Wow, what a show!

Map of North America

This is a map of North America. Alaska is one of the 50 states.

Color the state of Alaska red.

Color the rest of the United States yellow. Alaska and Hawaii are part of the United States and should also be colored yellow.

Color Canada green. Color Mexico blue.

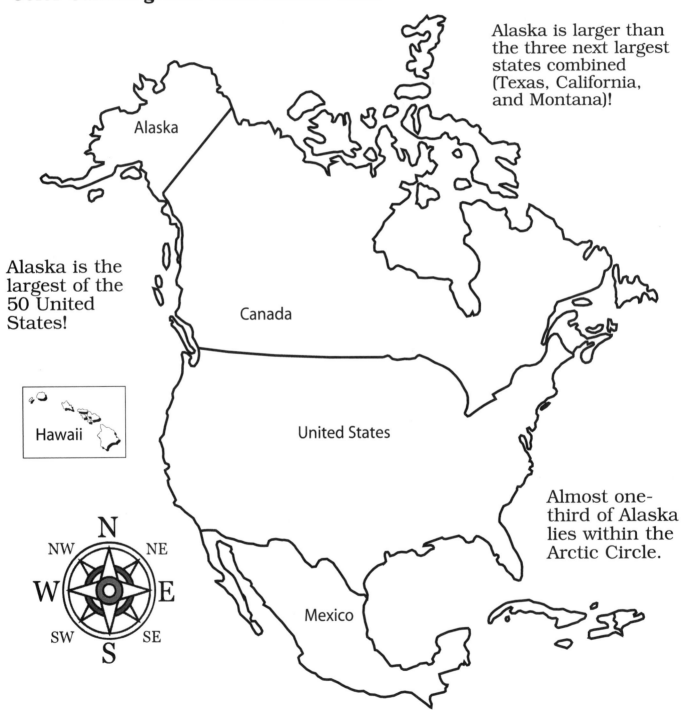

Alaska is larger than the three next largest states combined (Texas, California, and Montana)!

Alaska

Alaska is the largest of the 50 United States!

Canada

Hawaii

United States

Almost one-third of Alaska lies within the Arctic Circle.

N
NW   NE
W   E
SW   SE
S

Mexico

Is It True?

True or False?!

Alaska's diverse topography includes massive mountains, plateaus, more than 100,000 glaciers, lush rain forests, world's longest chain of active volcanoes, calderas, fjords, swamps, sea coasts, hot springs, and frozen Arctic plains. Bush is the name given to areas of wilderness, or areas that aren't accessible by roads.

No trees can grow on the Arctic Coastal Plain. In some areas, the ground thaws just enough for wildflowers, mosses, and short grasses to grow. These areas are called tundra. Permafrost is ground that's been frozen for two years or more. The Arctic Coastal Plain is permanent permafrost!

Read each sentence, and decide if it is TRUE or FALSE. Write your answers on the lines provided.

1. Alaska has about 1,000 glaciers. _____

2. The world's longest chain of active volcanoes is in Alaska.
   _____

3. Shrub is the name given to wilderness or areas that aren't accessible by roads. _____

4. Lots of trees grow on the Arctic Coastal Plain.
   _____

5. Permafrost is ground that's been frozen for two years or more.
   _____

ANSWERS: 1-False; 2-True; 3-False; 4-False; 5-True

Alaska State Great!

In the paragraph about an important person from Alaska below there are eight misspelled words. Circle the misspelled words, and then spell them correctly on the lines provided.

In 1976, student Molly Hootch goes to cort and wins! She fights for the wright to continue her education in her own vllage. Before Molly's fghit, students form many rural areas have to leaf home to attend hi school. Now all high school-age students are entitled to attend public schools in there own villages!

_____   _____

_____   _____

_____   _____

_____   _____

ANSWERS: cort, court; wright, right; vllage, village; fghit, fight; form, from; leaf, leave; hi, high; there, their

Virtual Alaska!

It's time to build your own website! We've given you pictures of things that have to do with Alaska. Color and cut them out, and arrange them on a blank piece of paper to create a web page that will make people want to visit Alaska!

The Call of the Wild!

American writer, Jack London is remembered for his vivid stories set in the Yukon. The novels are exciting and full of adventure. His stories tell of men and dogs struggling against nature and against each other!

In one of Jack London's classic tales titled *The Call of the Wild*, his hero, Buck, is a big dog stolen from his home and forced to live and struggle to survive as an Alaskan sled dog.

Buck does learn to survive but becomes too savage to live with people. He leaves the company of men and goes to live in the wild eventually taking over as leader of a wolf pack.

Throughout his stories, Jack London expresses his admiration for characters with the strength and courage to struggle against the odds and survive!

Read each sentence, and decide if it is FACT or FICTION. Write your answers on the lines provided.

1. Jack London was an American writer who wrote tales of the Yukon. _____

2. Buck was a big dog stolen from his home. _____

3. Buck was forced to work as an Alaskan sled dog. _____

4. Jack London admired strength and courage. _____

5. Buck became the leader of a wolf pack. _____

ANSWERS: 1-Fact; 2-Fiction; 3-Fiction; 4-Fact; 5-Fiction

Nifty Names!

Alaska has some great places with cool names! Let's take a tour!

Check out the clues and fill in the blanks!

WORD BANK

Banks	Fairweather
Bear	Gore
Clear	Icy
Cook	Lookout
Dry	Whale
East	

1. Brrrr! It's _ _ _ cold this morning!

2. On a _ _ _ _ _ day you can see forever!

3. Get the _ _ _ _ to fix us some lunch.

4. My goodness! It's a great big grizzly _ _ _ _

5. Where some folks keep their money: _ _ _ _ _ _

6. I need something to drink! My throat's as _ _ _ as it can be!

7. North, South, _ _ _ _, or West! Let's get started! Which way is best?

8. Yuck! That movie was full of blood, guts, and _ _ _ _!

9. Ahhh! What lovely _ _ _ _ _ _ _ _ _ _ _ we're having!

10. _ _ _ _ _ _ _! That's one really big _ _ _ _ _!

Alaska Firsts!

Extra, Extra, read all about it!
First newspaper, *The Alaska Times,* is published in 1869.

We can drive all the way?
In 1942, Alaska Highway becomes the first overland route to Lower 48 states.

Thar's gold in them thar hills!
Gold was first discovered near Sitka in 1872.

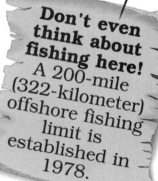

All aboard!
Alaska Marine Highway begins operation in 1963.

Don't even think about fishing here!
A 200-mile (322-kilometer) offshore fishing limit is established in 1978.

Tap into the reserves!
In 1998, falling oil prices force Alaska to use budget reserves.

Which "first" happened first?

Oil prices fall.

Gold!

Fishing limit established.

The first "first" is: _____

Alaska Gazetteer

A gazetteer is a list of places. For each of these famous Alaska places, write down the town in which it's located, and one interesting fact about the place. You may have to use an encyclopedia, almanac, or other resource to find the information, so dig deep!

1. Chilkoot Trail _____
   _____

2. Valley of Ten Thousand Smokes _____
   _____

3. Governor's Mansion _____
   _____

4. Alaska Totems _____
   _____

5. Alaska State Library _____
   _____

6. American Bald Eagle Foundation _____
   _____

7. Koyukuk National Wildlife Refuge _____
   _____

8. Alaskaland _____
   _____

WORD BANK

Anchorage	Juneau
Fairbanks	Katmai
Galena	Ketchikan
Haines	Skagway

ANSWERS: 1-Chilkoot Trail, Skagway; 2-Valley of Ten Thousand Smokes, Katmai; 3-Governor's Mansion, Juneau; 4- Alaska Totems, Ketchikan; 5- Alaska State Library, Anchorage; 6-American Bald Eagle Foundation, Haines; 7-Koyukuk National Wildlife Refuge, Galena; 8-Alaskaland, Fairbanks

Bio Bottles

Biography bottles are 2 or 3 liter bottles, emptied and cleaned. They are then decorated like your favorite Alaska character. They can represent a Musher, a Sourdough, or a Prospector. Use your imagination!

Here are some items you may want to help you:

☛ 2 or 3 liter bottles

☛ scissors

☛ glue

☛ felt

☛ balloon or styrofoam ball for head

☛ paint

☛ yarn for hair

Alaska Timeline!

A timeline is a list of important events and the year that they happened. You can use a timeline to understand more about history.

Read the timeline about Alaska history, then see if you can answer the questions at the bottom.

1741	Explorers Bering and Chirikov sight Alaska
1743	Russians hunt sea otters in Alaska for their fur
1774-94	Spain and England explore Alaskan waters
1784	Russians establish settlement on Kodiak Island
1853	Oil found in Cook Inlet
1867	William Henry Seward negotiates purchase of Alaska from Russia; United States buys Alaska for $7.2 million
1872	Gold discovered near Sitka
1959	Alaska becomes 49th state
1963	Alaska Marine Highway begins operation
1978	More than 58 million acres (23 million hectares) set aside for national monuments

Now put yourself back in the proper year if you were the following people.

1. If you are an explorer from Spain and are packing for a trip to explore Alaskan waters, the years are _____.
2. If you just got rich by striking oil, the year is _____.
3. If you are celebrating Alaska becoming the 49th state, the year is

   _____.
4. If you've just negotiated the sale of Alaska to the United States, the year is _____.
5. If you've just sighted Alaska from the deck of your ship, the year is _____.
6. If you're off to hunt sea otters, the year is _____.
7. If you're a prospector "stampeding" your way to the gold rush, the year is _____.
8. If you're a settler on Kodiak Island, the year is _____.

ANSWERS: 1-1774-1794; 2-1853; 3-1959; 4-1867; 5-1741; 6-1743; 7-1872; 8-1784

Alaska State Economy!

Alaska banks provide essential financial services. Some of the services that banks provide include:

- They lend money to consumers to purchase goods and services such as houses, cars, and education.
- They lend money to producers who start new businesses.
- They issue credit cards.
- They provide savings accounts and pay interest to savers.
- They provide checking accounts.

Circle whether you would have more, less, or the same amount of money after each event.

1. You deposit your paycheck into your checking account.   MORE   LESS   SAME

2. You put $1,000 in your savings account.   MORE   LESS   SAME

3. You use your credit card to buy new school clothes.   MORE   LESS   SAME

4. You borrow money from the bank to open a toy store.   MORE   LESS   SAME

5. You write a check at the grocery store.   MORE   LESS   SAME

6. You transfer money from checking to savings.   MORE   LESS   SAME

The biggest employer in Alaska is the U.S. government. The second largest is state and local governments.

These jobs include managing national and state park lands and staffing native community organizations.

ANSWERS: 1-more; 2-more; 3-less; 4-more; 5-less; 6-same

I Am A Famous Person From Alaska

From the Word Bank, find my name and fill in the blank.

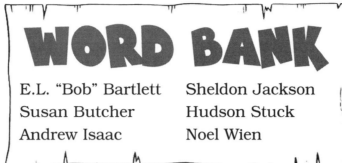

WORD BANK

E.L. "Bob" Bartlett   Sheldon Jackson

Susan Butcher   Hudson Stuck

Andrew Isaac   Noel Wien

1. I was an educator and missionary. In 1884, I came to Alaska to establish a Presbyterian mission. I worked to improve declining conditions of Alaska Natives and imported reindeer from Siberia to use for food and clothing.
Who am I? _____

2. I was chief of the United Crow Band and honored traditional ways of my people, but emphasized the value of education. I fought against drug and alcohol use among Alaska Natives.
Who am I? _____

3. I was a territorial delegate to U.S. Congress who fought for statehood. I was one of Alaska's first state senators after statehood. My Fur Seal Act of 1966 granted Aleuts local government powers.
Who am I? _____

4. I was an Episcopalian missionary who fought to protect the Native Alaskans' way of life. In 1913, I led the first expedition to reach the tallest peak of Mount McKinley.
Who am I? _____

5. I am a four-time winner of Iditarod. I'm the first person ever to win three Iditarod races in a row.
Who am I? _____

6. I was a legendary bush pilot with an excellent sense of direction. I never got lost! I pioneered many flight routes. I was the first man to fly north of the Arctic Circle and the first to operate an airline through the winter in the Arctic. I formed Wien Alaska Airlines with my brother Ralph.
Who am I? _____

Ancient Artifacts
In Alaska!

Alaska's earliest residents were the Eskimo, Indian, and Aleut peoples. Each ethnic group had its own distinct culture. Today, Alaska Natives, numbering more than 100,000, make up about 17 percent of the state's population. Although some Alaska Natives live in the cities, many live a subsistence life using traditional methods to hunt, gather, and fish.

You are an archaeologist digging into the Dry Creek archeological site near Healy. Below are pictures of some of the artifacts that you find. Now, you have to identify these strange objects and their uses.

Write down what you think these artifacts are used for!

_____

_____

_____

_____

_____

_____

_____

_____

_____

_____

_____

_____

_____

_____

_____

Native Alaskans!

When the settlers arrived, there were several Native Alaskan groups already living in Alaska. Aleuts and Eskimos lived along the northwest coast and in the Aleutian Islands and fished the coastal waters. Alaskan Eskimos are related to the large Eskimo populations of Siberia, Canada, and Greenland and are collectively known as Inuit.

The Athabascan Indians lived a semi-nomadic life in the interior. They hunted moose, caribou, and waterfowl and followed the animals as they migrated from place to place.

Tlingit and Haida Indians lived in permanent settlements in southeast Alaska. The food was plentiful and the climate was milder.

Draw a line from the group to its location on the map.

Aleuts   Tlingit Indians

Haida Indians   Inuit

Athabascan Indians

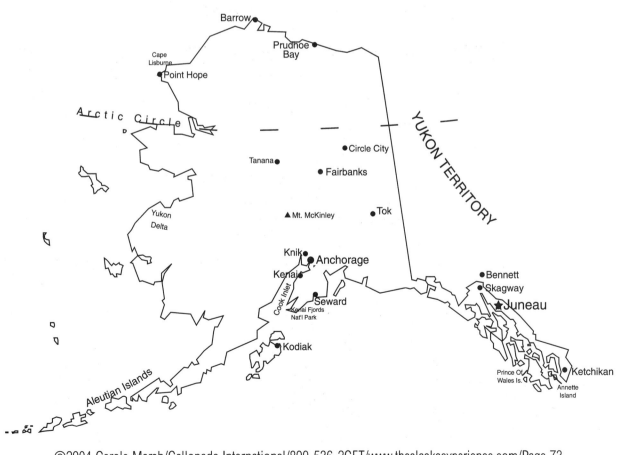

IT'S MONEY IN THE BANK!!

You spent the summer drilling in the Prudhoe Bay oil fields, and you made a lot of money...$500 to be exact!

Solve the math problems below.

TOTAL EARNED: $500.00

I will pay back my Mom this much for money I borrowed when I first started working. Thanks, Mom!   A. $20.00

    subtract A from $500   B. _____

I will give my little brother this much money for taking my phone messages while I was at work: C. $10.00

    subtract C from B   D. _____

I will spend this much on a special treat or reward for myself: E. $25.00

    subtract E from D   F. _____

I will save this much for college: G. $300.00

    subtract G from F   H. _____

I will put this much in my new savings account so I can buy school clothes: I. $100.00

    subtract I from H   J. _____

TOTAL STILL AVAILABLE   (use answer J) _____

TOTAL SPENT   (add A, C, and E) _____

Great Cities Word Search!

Find the names of these Alaska cities in the Word Search below:

WORD BANK

Anchorage
Barrow
Bethel
College
Fairbanks
Juneau
Ketchikan

Kodiak
Kotzebue
Nome
Petersburg
Seward
Unalaska
Wrangell

```
K S K N A B R I A F E S P B D
C A L R A G I N M M W H E R B
A C I D K K C K O C Z U T U J
F I O D P H I N B A K B E U T
U O T L O V Z H Z L E U R D Q
O S Y R L K W B C U Q Y S P R
W R A N G E L L B T O D B P D
M G A I O D G E B S E G U K R
E E K A H J Z E A G Y K R F A
A H S F N T Q X R C W F G B W
T C A L O T L R R D R B E T E
F T L K A O Z Z O V X T F Z S
H K A X H F I P W K H T G K P
R J N U G H W K K E E M A L R
L Z U E X Q S B L U A E N U J
```

Numbering The Alaskans!

STATE OF ALASKA
CENSUS REPORT

Every ten years, it's time for Alaskans to stand up and be counted. Since 1790, the United States has conducted a census, or count, of each of its citizens. **Practice filling out a pretend census form.**

Name _____ Age ▢

Place of Birth _____

Current Address _____

Does your family own or rent where you live? _____

How long have you lived in Alaska? _____

How many people are in your family? _____

How many females? ▢ How many males? ▢

What are their ages? _____

How many rooms are in your house? ▢

How is your home heated? _____

How many cars does your family own? ▢

How many telephones are in your home? ▢

Is your home a farm? _____

Sounds pretty nosy, doesn't it? But a census is very important. The information is used for all kinds of purposes, including setting budgets, zoning land, determining how many schools to build, and much more. The census helps Alaska leaders plan for the future needs of its citizens. Hey, that's you!

Endangered And Threatened Alaska

Each state has a list of the endangered species found within its borders. An animal is labeled endangered when it is at risk of becoming extinct, or dying out completely.

Alaska's list of endangered species is very short! The state has long protected its wildlife and their habitats! Alaska stands out from the rest of the nation because it still has nearly all of its native animals and plants in abundance!

WORD BANK

Blue whale
Eskimo curlew
Humpback whale
Right whale
Short-tailed albatross

Can you help rescue these endangered and threatened animals by filling in their names below?

1. S _ _ _ _ - _ _ _ _ _ _   _ _ _ _ _ _ _ _ _

2. B _ _ _   W _ _ L _

3. _ _ _ _ B _ _ K   _ H _ _ E

4. _ S _ _ _ _   C _ _ _ _ W

5. _ _ G _ _   _ _ A _ _

Circle the animal that is extinct (not here anymore).

Sing A Sweet State Song!

"Alaska's Flag"

Eight stars of gold on a field of blue—Alaska's flag.
May it mean to you the blue of the sea, the evening sky,
The mountain lakes, and the flow'rs nearby;
The gold of the early sourdough's dreams,
The precious gold of the hills and streams;
The brilliant stars in the northern sky,
The "Bear"—the "Dipper"—and, shining high,
The great North Star with its steady light,
Over land and sea a beacon bright.
Alaska's flag—to Alaskans dear,
The simple flag of a last frontier.

Answer the following questions:

1. How many stars of gold are on a field of blue?
   _____

2. Name one thing the blue represents.
   _____

3. Who was dreaming about gold?
   _____

4. Which great star shines with a steady light?
   _____

5. What does the simple flag represent?
   _____

ANSWERS: 1-eight; 2-blue of the sea, evening sky, mountain lakes, flow'rs nearby (may vary slightly); 3-sourdoughs; 4-North Star; 5-Last Frontier

Getting Ready To Vote In Alaska!

When you turn 18, you will be eligible to vote. Your vote counts! Many elections have been won by just a few votes.

The following is a form for your personal voting information. You will need to do some research to get all the answers!

I will be eligible to vote on this date _____

I live in this Congressional District _____

I live in this State Senate District _____

I live in this State Representative District _____

The first local election I can vote in will be _____

The first state election I can vote in will be _____

The first national election I can vote in will be _____

The governor of our state is _____

One of my state senators is _____

One of my state representatives is _____

The local public office I would like to run for is _____

The state public office I would like to run for is _____

The federal public office I would like to run for is _____

Did you know that our state government has 20 senators?

The number of legislators may change after each census.

No, but I do know we have 40 representatives!

The Alaska State Seal

The state seal of Alaska features mountains and the northern lights, a symbol for mining, a train, trees, a farmer and his horse, wheat, and fish.

FAST FACTS:
Alaska's state motto is "North to the Future." The state motto refers to Alaska as a land of promise!

Color the state seal.

The state seal of Alaska was designed in 1910 while Alaska was still a territory.

Alaska State Symbol Scramble!

**Unscramble the names of these symbols for the state of Alaska.
Write the answers in the word wheel around the picture of each symbol.**

1. **L O W W I L   N A G I M R A T P** Hint: A pheasant-like bird that lives in willows and on the open tundra. In summer, the feathers are mostly chestnut brown but turn snowy white in the winter.
2. **K A S I T   P R S U C E** Hint: The biggest and fastest-growing of all the spruce trees.
3. **N T O - E M - T O G R E F** Hint: The wild was adopted as the state flower in 1917. The beautiful blue flowers have yellow centers and can be found throughout Alaska.
4. **S O O M E** Hint: The largest members of the deer family.
5. **W O B H E A D   L A W H E** Hint: This mammal "summers" in the Arctic Ocean and spends its winters in the Bering and Chukchi Seas.

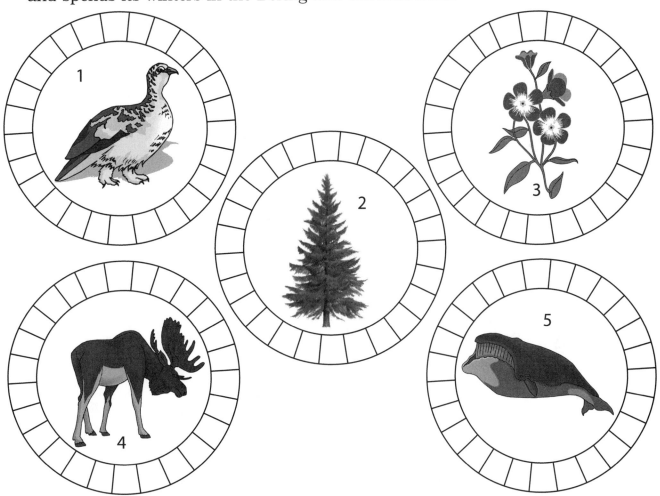

A Quilt Of Many Boroughs

Alaska has 16 organized boroughs. Much of Alaska is considered an "unorganized borough." Alaska is divided into 27 census areas.

– **Label your census area. Color it red.**
– **Label your neighboring census areas. Color them blue.**
– **Now color the rest of the census areas green.**

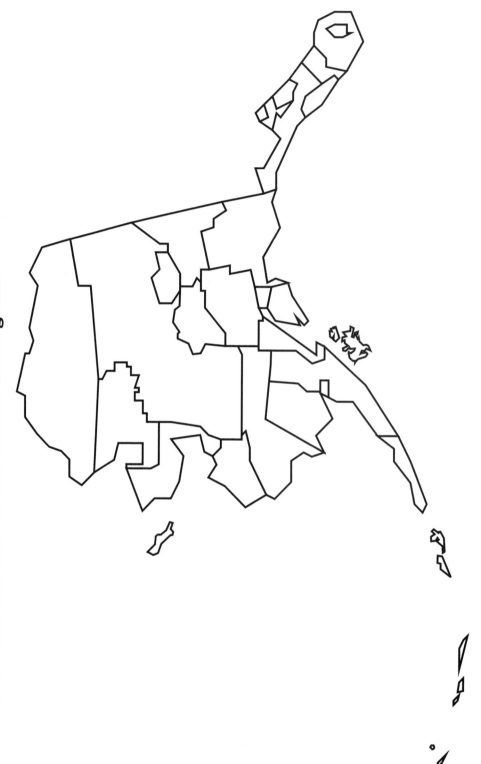

World At War!

The United States entered World War II in 1941 after Japanese forces attacked the American military base at Pearl Harbor in the Hawaiian Islands. In 1942, Japanese troops bombed Dutch Harbor in the Aleutian Islands and occupied Kiska Island and Attu Island. Kiska and Attu islands were the only part of North America invaded during World War II.

Americans went into action! They built the Alaska Highway in 1942 as a military supply road. In 1943, about 152,000 American military troops were stationed in Alaska. They fought the Japanese and recovered Kiska and Attu islands. The world war in Alaska was over!

Read each statement about the war in Alaska and decide whether the statement is a FACT or an OPINION. Write your answer on the line.

1. The United States entered World War II in 1941.

   _____

2. World War II was the worst war ever!

   _____

3. Japanese forces bombed Dutch Harbor in 1942.

   _____

4. Kiska and Attu islands were the only part of North America invaded during World War II.

   _____

5. The Japanese invaded the United States because they were mad at the Americans!

   _____

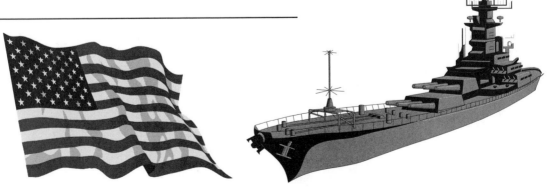

Mush!

Dog **mushing**, or sled dog racing, is Alaska's **official** state sport. Dogs and their people race during the winter. Some races are about speed! Some are about distance and **surviving** the elements! Some races have teams of 3 to 10 dogs. Others have no limits on the number of dogs.

The Iditarod Trail Sled Dog Race and the Yukon Quest International Sled Dog Race are two of the most famous, long-distance championship races. The Iditarod followed the old dog team mail route from Knik to Nome. The trail was lengthened to 1,100 miles (1,770 kilometers) with the starting line in Anchorage! The U.S. Congress **designated** the Iditarod a National **Historic** Trail in 1976.

Survival becomes more important than winning if a team gets caught in a winter storm. Mushers will often stop to help another team and give up their chance to win.

See if you can figure out the meanings of these words from the story above.

1. mushing:
_____

2. official:
_____

3. surviving:
_____

4. designated:
_____

5. historic:
_____

HINT: You may need to look for root words!

Now check your answers in a dictionary. How close did you get to the real definitions?

Which Founding Person Am I?

From the Word Bank, find my name and fill in the blank.

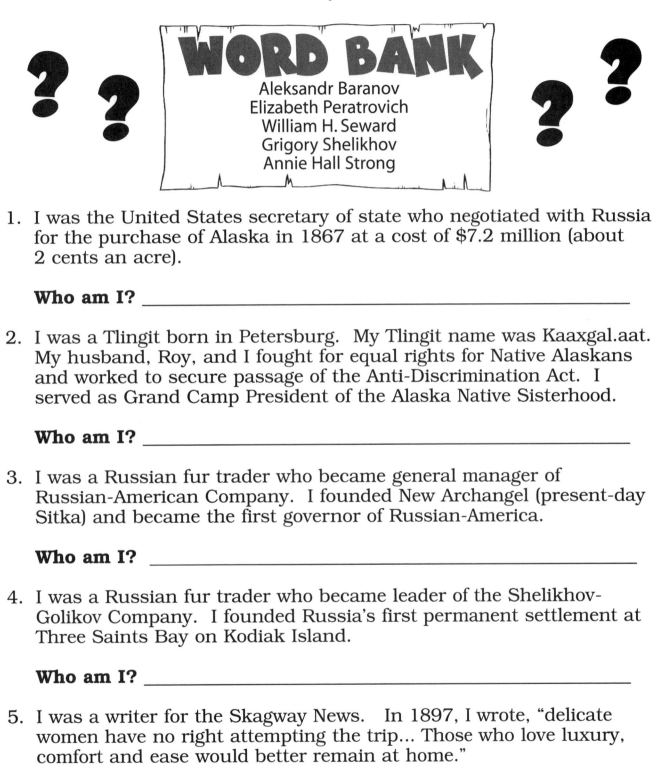

WORD BANK

Aleksandr Baranov
Elizabeth Peratrovich
William H. Seward
Grigory Shelikhov
Annie Hall Strong

1. I was the United States secretary of state who negotiated with Russia for the purchase of Alaska in 1867 at a cost of $7.2 million (about 2 cents an acre).

   Who am I? _____

2. I was a Tlingit born in Petersburg. My Tlingit name was Kaaxgal.aat. My husband, Roy, and I fought for equal rights for Native Alaskans and worked to secure passage of the Anti-Discrimination Act. I served as Grand Camp President of the Alaska Native Sisterhood.

   Who am I? _____

3. I was a Russian fur trader who became general manager of Russian-American Company. I founded New Archangel (present-day Sitka) and became the first governor of Russian-America.

   Who am I? _____

4. I was a Russian fur trader who became leader of the Shelikhov-Golikov Company. I founded Russia's first permanent settlement at Three Saints Bay on Kodiak Island.

   Who am I? _____

5. I was a writer for the Skagway News. In 1897, I wrote, "delicate women have no right attempting the trip... Those who love luxury, comfort and ease would better remain at home."

   Who am I? _____

ANSWERS: 1-William H. Seward; 2-Elizabeth Peratrovich; 3-Aleksandr Baranov; 4-Grigory Shelikhov; 5-Annie Hall Strong

!! It Could Happen— And It Did! !!

These historical events from Alaska's past are all out of order. Can you put them back together in the correct order? Number these events from 1 to 10, beginning with the earliest. (There's a great big hint at the end of each sentence.)

_____ U.S. Congress declares territorial status for Alaska. (1912)

_____ Bering and Chirikov sight Alaska. (1741)

_____ Alaska Marine Highway begins operation. (1963)

_____ Alaska becomes 49th state. (1959)

_____ Oil is found in Cook Inlet. (1853)

_____ More than 58 million acres (23 million hectares) are set aside for national monuments. (1978)

_____ Gold is discovered near Sitka. (1872)

_____ Alaska Native Claims Settlement Act grants title to 40 million acres (16 million hectares) of land and provides $900 million in payment. (1971)

_____ Alaska Permanent Fund created from mineral oil lease proceeds (oil). Annual dividends are paid to qualifying residents. (1976)

_____ Alaska National Interest Lands Conservation Act transfers 53.7 million acres (21.7 million hectares) to national wildlife refuge system. (1980)

ANSWERS: will appear in this order: 4; 1; 6; 5; 2; 9; 3; 7; 8; 10

Wild, Woolly Mammoths!

Woolly mammoths (*Mammuthus primigenius*) roamed Alaska 10,000 years ago, even after people crossed the Bering Strait from Asia. Woolly mammoths could still be seen on Wrangell Island (off the coast of Siberia) up until 4,000 years ago!

A large woolly mammoth was 9 feet (3 meters) high at the shoulder (about the size of a modern-day elephant). They were covered with long hair and had curved tusks as long as 16 feet (5 meters). The tremendous tusks helped move the snow and ice to uncover their meals of tundra plants. Yum!

Several woolly mammoths were recovered in Alaska. The best known, nicknamed "Blue Babe," was found near Fairbanks. It's still there—on display at the University of Alaska Museum.

Below is a picture of a woolly mammoth. Using the information above, label how tall he is at the shoulder and the length of his curved tusks. Be sure and include the metric measurements. Then, circle the types of food that woolly mammoths would eat.

Length_____

Height_____

ANSWERS: 9 feet (3 meters) high at the shoulder; curved tusks as long as 16 feet (5 meters)

Alaska Word Wheel—Give It Another Spin!

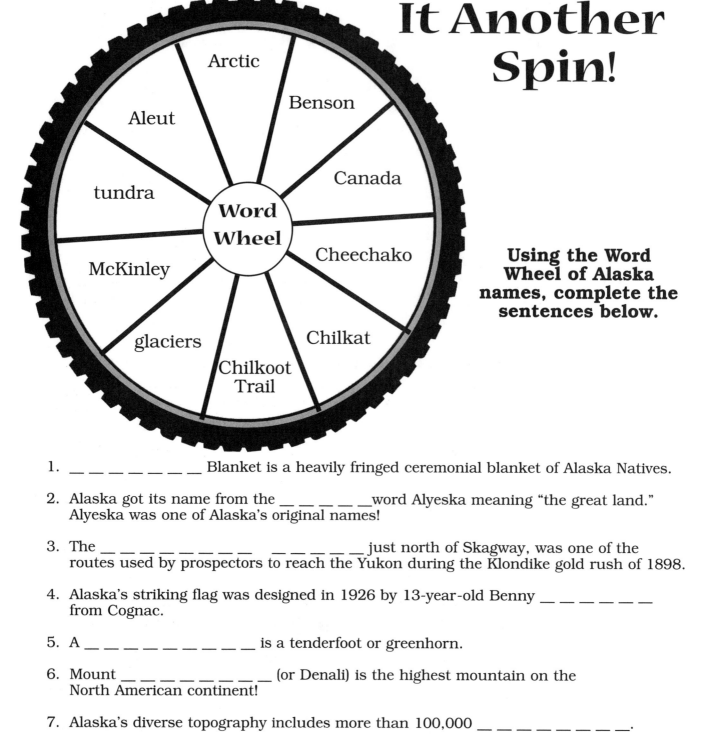

Using the Word Wheel of Alaska names, complete the sentences below.

1. _ _ _ _ _ _ _ Blanket is a heavily fringed ceremonial blanket of Alaska Natives.

2. Alaska got its name from the _ _ _ _ _word Alyeska meaning "the great land." Alyeska was one of Alaska's original names!

3. The _ _ _ _ _ _ _ _ _ _ _ _ _ _ just north of Skagway, was one of the routes used by prospectors to reach the Yukon during the Klondike gold rush of 1898.

4. Alaska's striking flag was designed in 1926 by 13-year-old Benny _ _ _ _ _ _ _ from Cognac.

5. A _ _ _ _ _ _ _ _ _ _ is a tenderfoot or greenhorn.

6. Mount _ _ _ _ _ _ _ _ _ (or Denali) is the highest mountain on the North American continent!

7. Alaska's diverse topography includes more than 100,000 _ _ _ _ _ _ _ _.

8. No trees can grow on the _ _ _ _ _ _ Coastal Plain.

9. On the _ _ _ _ _ _ _, the ground thaws just enough for wildflowers, mosses, and short grasses to grow.

10. Alaska's neighbor to the east is _ _ _ _ _ _ _.

Alaska Pop Quiz!

Pop quiz! It's time to test your knowledge of Alaska!

Try to answer all of the questions before you look at the answers.

1. Ground that's been frozen for two years or more is called:
   a. frost free
   b. permafrost
   c. sort of frozen

2. Mount McKinley was originally called *Denali*, or _____ by Alaska Natives.
   a. Mountain with Two Peaks
   b. The Great One
   c. The Big One that's really hard to climb

3. How many rivers does Alaska have?
   a. more than 3,000
   b. more than 30,000
   c. more than 300,000

4. What are Bunny Boots?
   a. boots designed to protect feet in sub-zero temperatures
   b. little shoes Arctic hares wear
   c. shoes that all Alaska tourists are required to wear

5. Ninety-four of Alaska's lakes are bigger than:
   a. a bread box
   b. 1,000 square miles (2,590 square kilometers)
   c. 10 square miles (26 square kilometers)

6. The White Pass & Yukon Railroad travels the historic _____ to British Columbia, Canada.
   a. road less traveled
   b. mail route
   c. gold rush route

7. Alaska is sixth in the nation in number of airports. Much of Alaska's interior travel is provided by:
   a. bush planes, seaplanes, and helicopters
   b. buses
   c. taxicabs

8. William Henry Seward negotiated the purchase of Alaska from Russia in what year?
   a. 1867
   b. 1678
   c. 1768

9. Alaska Day is celebrated every October 18. It commemorates what event?
   a. purchase of Alaska by United States
   b. formal transfer of the territory and raising of the U.S. flag
   c. date Alaska was first settled by Russian explorers

10. In 1880, Joe Juneau and Dick Harris struck it rich near present-day Juneau. What did they strike?
    a. oil
    b. jade
    c. gold

ANSWERS: 1-b; 2-b; 3-a; 4-a; 5-c; 6-c; 7-a; 8-a; 9-b; 10-c

Languages Of Native Alaska!

    Eskimo languages are widely spoken across western and northern Alaska. They are Yupik, Central Yupik, Siberian Yupik, and Inupiaq. There are more than 20 Native American languages spoken in Alaska. Fifteen are at risk of becoming extinct—of being heard no more. Aleuts are related to the Eskimo people but have their own language and culture. Most Alaska Natives speak English as well as their own language.

- *Barabara:* pronounced buh-RAH-buh-ruh is a dwelling built of sod.
- *Cheechako:* Chinook Indian word pronounced chee-CHA-ko is a greenhorn or tenderfoot, a newcomer.
- *Oogruk:* Eskimo name for the Pacific bearded seal, a staple food of subsistence hunters in the Far North
- *Nalukatak:* A traditional Eskimo game of blanket toss. A circle of people hold a walrus skin stretched tight. The person standing in the middle of the skin is tossed higher and higher until he or she no longer lands on his or her feet!

In each pair of sentences below, one of the statements is false. Read them carefully and choose the sentence that is not true. Cross out the false sentence, and circle the true sentence.

1. Alaskan Eskimo languages are widely spoken in southern Alaska. Eskimo languages are Yupik, Central Yupik, Siberian Yupik, and Inupiaq.

2. There are more than 20 Native American languages spoken in Alaska. Only five of these languages are in danger of becoming extinct.

3. Barabara is a house made of ice and snow. It is pronounced buh-RAH-buh-ruh.

4. *Cheechako* is a Cherokee Indian word. It means greenhorn or tenderfoot.

5. *Nalukatak* is a traditional Eskimo game of blanket toss. A person stands in the middle of a walrus skin and is tossed higher and higher until he or she asks to stop and get off.

ANSWERS: 1-first is false; 2-second is false; 3-first is false; 4-first is false; 5-second is false

Massive Mounds Of Mighty Mountains!

Alaska has 39 mountain ranges with 17 of the 20 highest peaks in the nation! Nineteen peaks are over 14,000 feet (4,267 meters).

- Mount McKinley: 20,320 feet (6,194 meters)
- Mount Saint Elias: 18,008 feet (5,489 meters)
- Mount Foraker: 17,400 feet (5,303 meters)
- Mount Bona: 16,500 feet (5,029 meters)
- Mount Blackburn: 16,390 feet (4,996 meters)
- Mount Sanford: 16,237 feet (4,949 meters)

Using the information above, graph the elevations (heights) of these mighty mountains The first one has been done for you.

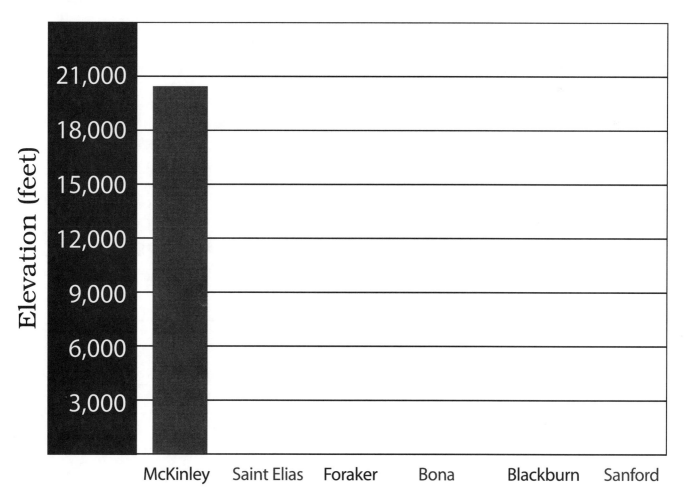

Land Of The Midnight Sun

Alaska is known as the "Land of the Midnight Sun." Does the sun really shine at midnight? Yes! When summer arrives (summer solstice), the North Pole tilts toward the sun, and the daylight lasts up to 24 hours! All that extra sunlight grows really BIG veggies!

The Arctic Circle is one interesting latitude! The sun never sets on the day of summer solstice and never rises on the day of winter solstice (when winter blows in). The latitude changes a little from year to year, but it's approximately 66°34' north. In Barrow, the northernmost point in Alaska and the United States, the sun does not set from May 10 to August 2. During the winter in Barrow, the sun does not rise for 67 days! The only "night light" is the moon and the glow of the northern lights!

A haiku is a three-line poem with a certain number of syllables in each line. **Look at the example below:**

The first line has 5 syllables
Land/of/Mid/night/Sun

The second line has 7 syllables
Lots/of/light/and/lots/of/fun!

The third line has 5 syllables
This/is/how/it's/done!

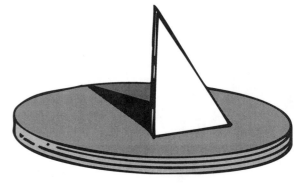

**Now, write your own haiku about the amazing
Land of the Midnight Sun!**

_____

_____

_____

Many Rivers Flow Through It!

The state of Alaska is blessed with more than 3,000 rivers! The longest is the Yukon River that rushes for 1,400 miles (2,253 kilometers) through Alaska. And it doesn't stop there! The Yukon flows on into Canada.

Many of Alaska's rivers have been designated wild and scenic by the U.S. government. The National Wild and Scenic Rivers System protects rivers of great beauty or those that have recreational, historic, cultural, or ecological value.

River	Distance
Yukon River	1,400 miles (2,253 kilometers)
Porcupine River	555 miles (893 kilometers)
Koyukuk River	554 miles (892 kilometers)
Kuskokwim River	540 miles (869 kilometers)
Tanana River	531 miles (855 kilometers)
Innoko River	463 miles (745 kilometers)
Colville River	428 miles (689 kilometers)
Noatak River	396 miles (637 kilometers)
Kobuk River	396 miles (637 kilometers)
Birch Creek	314 miles (505 kilometers)

Check out the chart to find answers to these questions.

1. The longest river in Alaska is the __ __ __ __ __   __ __ __ __ __.

2. The shortest river shown on the chart is __ __ __ __ __   __ __ __ __ __
   that flows for __ __ __ miles (__ __ __ kilometers).

3. The __ __ __ __ __ __ __ __ __ River is 555 miles (893 kilometers) long.

4. The Tanana River is __ __ __ miles (__ __ __ kilometers) long.

5. Which river is closest to 450 miles (724 kilometers) long?
   __ __ __ __ __ __ River

ANSWERS: 1-Yukon River; 2-Birch Creek, 314, 505; 3-Porcupine; 4-531, 855; 5-Innoko River

How Big is Alaska?

With a total area of approximately 615,230 square miles (1,593,323 square kilometers), Alaska is the largest of the 50 United States! When a scale map of Alaska is placed over a scale map of the contiguous United States, Alaska extends from coast to coast of the Lower 48!

Can you answer the following questions?

1. How many states are there in the United States?

   _____

2. This many states are smaller than our state:

   _____

3. This many states are larger than our state:

   _____

4. One mile = 5,280 _____ _____ _____ _____

   HINT:

5. Draw a square foot.

6. Classroom Challenge: After you have drawn a square foot, measure the number of square feet in your classroom. Most floor tiles are square feet (12 inches by 12 inches). How many square feet are in your classroom? _____

   Bonus: Try to calculate how many classrooms would fit in the total area of your state. _____

   Hint: About 46,464 average classrooms would fit in just one square mile!

Grand And Glorious Glaciers!

Alaska has more than 100,000 glaciers that range in size from tiny to tremendous! Alaska's glaciers fall into five categories: alpine, ice caps, ice fields, piedmont, and valley.

What causes a glacier to form? It's when more snow falls than melts—over a number of years. Malaspina Glacier is the largest glacier in North America! It starts in the St. Elias Mountains, covers about 1,500 square miles (4,075 square kilometers), and ends between Yakutat Bay and Icy Bay in Southeast. That's bigger than the state of Rhode Island.

Some of Alaska's best-known glaciers include Bering, Worthington, Matanuska, Exit, Portage, and Mendenhall.

Answer the following questions:

1. How many glaciers are in Alaska?

   _____

2. Are all glaciers the same size?

   _____

3. What color does glacier ice often appear to the eye?

   _____

4. What causes a glacier to form?

   _____

5. What is Alaska's largest glacier?

   _____

Frosty Facts:
- Glacier ice often appears blue to the eye
- About three-quarters of all the fresh water in Alaska is "stored" as glacial ice
- Alaska has more than 750 glacier-dammed lakes
- Tidewater glaciers calve or "form" icebergs by "delivering" masses of broken ice

ANSWERS: 1-more than 100,000; 2-no; 3-blue; 4-when more snow falls than melts-over a number of years; 5-Malaspina Glacier

"A" Is For Alaska

The words below are known as an *acrostic*. See if you can make up your own acrostic poem describing Alaska. For each letter in Alaska's name, write down a word or phrase that describes Alaska. The first is done for you.

A is for <u>is for the Aleut word Alyeska meaning "the great land."</u>

L is for _____

A is for _____

S is for _____

K is for _____

A is for _____

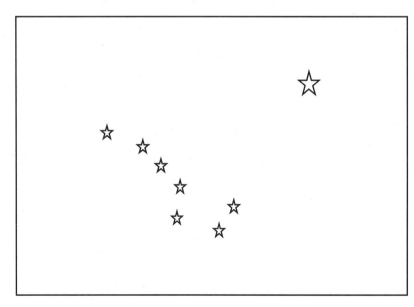